International Kierkegaard
Commentary

International Kierkegaard Commentary:
The Concept of Anxiety

edited by
Robert L. Perkins

MERCER

ISBN 0-86554-142-6

IKC: The Concept of Anxiety
Copyright © 1985
Mercer University Press, Macon, Georgia 31207
All rights reserved
Printed in the United States of America

All books published by Mercer University Press
are produced on acid-free paper that exceeds
the minimum standards established by the
National Historical Publications and Records Commission.

Library of Congress Cataloging-in-Publication Data

Main entry under title:

The Concept of anxiety.
(International Kierkegaard commentary ; 8)
Includes index.
    1. Kierkegaard, Søren, 1813–1855. Begrebet angest—
Addresses, essays, lectures. 2. Sin, original—
History of doctrines—19th century—Addresses, essays,
lectures. 3. Psychology, Religious—History—19th
century—Addresses, essays, lectures. 4. Anxiety—
Religious aspects—Christianity—History—19th century—
Addresses, essays, lectures. I. Perkins, Robert L.,
1930–   . II. Title.

B4376.I58   1984 vol. 8   198'.9 s   85-11571
[BT720]   [233'.14]
ISBN 0-86554-142-6 (alk. paper)

Contents

out

Acknowledgments

All the contributors to this volume would desire to make acknowledgments, but it is a privilege reserved for the editor. Those whom the contributors would have named will be satisfied to have served their friends and colleagues. I am sure each would name persons who have the same functions as my friends and colleagues.

I am appreciative of the numerous persons named in the first volume published in this series, *International Kierkegaard Commentary: Two Ages*, at the University of South Alabama. However, due to a professional move, I have the privilege of thanking a number of additional persons at Stetson University: Pope A. Duncan, President; Denton R. Coker, Provost; H. Graves Edmondson, Vice-President for Business and Finance; Richard E. Wright and Mary E. McBride of Data Processing. My executive secretary, Susan S. Johnson, has made getting into this deanship easier in a thousand ways and has helped me save many hours to bring the editing process to a conclusion.

The Advisory Board and the Volume Consultant read the volume, and their recommendations considerably improve it. The International Advisory Board has offered valuable advice on a number of matters. Robert C. Roberts and Sylvia I. Walsh read some of the essays and made valuable suggestions for improvements.

The interest of Mercer University Press is appreciated.

Princeton University Press granted permission to quote from *The Concept of Anxiety* and other copyrighted materials.

Last but hardly least, the several contributors and the editor thank their families for the lost evenings and other scattered hours.

Robert L. Perkins

Sigla

CI *The Concept of Irony*, trans. Lee Capel. New York: Harper and Row, 1966; Bloomington: Indiana University Press, 1968. (*Om Begrebet Ironi*, by S. Kierkegaard, 1841.)

EO *Either/Or*, vol. 1, trans. David F. Swenson and Lillian Marvin Swenson, vol. 2, trans. Walter Lowrie, 2d ed., rev. Howard A. Johnson. Princeton: Princeton University Press, 1971. (*Enten-Eller*, 1-2, ed. Victor Eremita, 1843.)

JC *Johannes Climacus or De omnibus dubitandum est* and *A Sermon*, trans. T. H. Croxall. London: Adam and Charles Black, 1958. ("Johannes Climacus eller *De omnibus dubitandum est*," written 1842-1843, unpubl., *Papirer* IV B 1; "Demis-Prædiken," 1844, unpubl., *Papirer* IV C 1.)

ED *Edifying Discourses*, 1-4, trans. David F. Swenson and Lillian Marvin Swenson. Minneapolis: Augsburg Publishing House, 1943-1946. (*Opbyggelige Taler*, by S. Kierkegaard, 1843, 1844.)

FT *Fear and Trembling*, trans. Walter Lowrie. Princeton: Princeton University Press, 1968. (*Frygt og Bæven*, by Johannes De Silentio, 1843.)

R *Repetition*, trans. Walter Lowrie. Princeton: Princeton University Press, 1941. (*Gjentagelsen*, by Constantin Constantius, 1843.)

PF *Philosophical Fragments*, trans. David Swenson, 2d ed., rev. Howard Hong. Princeton: Princeton University Press, 1980. (*Philosophiske Smuler*, by Johannes Climacus, ed. S. Kierkegaard, 1844.)

CA *The Concept of Anxiety*, trans. Reidar Thomte and Albert B. Anderson. Princeton: Princeton University Press, 1980. (*Begrebet Angest*, by Vigilius Haufniensis, ed. S. Kierkegaard, 1844.)

TCS *Three Discourses on Imagined Occasions [Thoughts on Crucial Situations in Human Life]*, trans. David F. Swenson, ed. Lillian Marvin Swenson. Minneapolis: Augsburg Publishing House, 1941. (*Tre Taler vedtænkte Leiligheder*, by S. Kierkegaard, 1845.)

SLW *Stages on Life's Way*, trans. Walter Lowrie. Princeton: Princeton University Press, 1940. (*Stadier paa Livets Vej*, ed. Hilarius Bogbinder, 1845.)

CUP *Concluding Unscientific Postscript*, trans. David F. Swenson and Walter Lowrie. Princeton: Princeton University Press for American-Scandinavian Foundation, 1941. (*Afsluttende uvidenskabelig Efterskrift*, by Johannes Climacus, ed. S. Kierkegaard, 1846.)

TA *Two Ages: The Age of Revolution and the Present Age. A Literary Review*, trans. Howard V. Hong and Edna H. Hong. Princeton: Princeton University Press, 1978. (*En literair Anmeldelse. To Tidsaldre*, by S. Kierkegaard, 1846.)

OAR *On Authority and Revelation, The Book on Adler*, trans. Walter Lowrie. Princeton: Princeton University Press, 1955. (*Bogen om Adler*, written 1846-1847, unpubl., *Papirer* VII² B 235; VIII² B 1-27.)

PH *Edifying Discourses in Various Spirits*. (*Opbyggelige Taler i forskjellig Aand*, by S. Kierkegaard, 1847.) Part One, *Purity of Heart ["En Leiligheds-Tale"]* 2d ed., trans. Douglas Steere. New York: Harper, 1948.

GS Part Three and Part Two, *The Gospel of Suffering* and *The Lilies of the Field ["Lidelsernes Evangelium"* and *"Lilierne paa Marken og Himlens Fugle"]*, trans. David F. Swenson and Lillian Marvin Swenson. Minneapolis: Augsburg Publishing House, 1948.

WL *Works of Love*, trans. Howard V. Hong and Edna H. Hong. New York: Harper and Row, 1962. (*Kjerlighedens Gjerninger*, by S. Kierkegaard, 1847.)

C *The Crisis [and a Crisis] in the Life of an Actress*, trans. Stephen Crites. New York: Harper and Row, 1967. (*Krisen og en Krise i en Skuespillerindes Liv*, by Inter et Inter. *Fædrelandet*, 188-91, 24-27 July 1848.)

CD *Christian Discourses*, including *The Lilies of the Field and the Birds of the Air* and *Three Discourses at the Communion on Fridays*, trans. Walter Lowrie. London and New York: Oxford University Press, 1940. (*Christelige Taler*, by S. Kierkegaard, 1848; *Lilien paa Marken og Fuglen under Himlen*, by S. Kierkegaard, 1849; *Tre Taler ved Altergangen om Fredagen*, by S. Kierkegaard, 1849.)

SUD *The Sickness unto Death*, trans. Howard V. Hong and Edna H. Hong. Princeton: Princeton University Press, 1980. (*Sygdommen til Doden*, by Anti-Climacus, ed S. Kierkegaard, 1849.)

TC *Training in Christianity*, including "The Woman Who Was a Sinner," trans. Walter Lowrie. London and New York: Oxford University Press, 1941; reprint, Princeton: Princeton University Press, 1944. (*Indovelse i Christendom*, by Anti-Climacus, ed. S. Kierkegaard, 1850; *En opbyggelig Tale*, by S. Kierkegaard, 1850.)

AN *Armed Neutrality* and *An Open Letter*, trans. Howard V. Hong and Edna H. Hong. Bloomington and London: Indiana University Press, 1968. (*Den bevæbnede Neutralitet*, written 1848-1849, publ. 1965; *Foranledigt ved en Yttring af Dr. Rudelbach mig betræffende, Fædrelandet*, no. 26, 31 January 1851.)

PV *The Point of View for My Work as an Author*, including the appendix " 'The Single Individual,' Two 'Notes' Concerning My Work as an Author," and *On My Work as an Author*, trans. Walter Lowrie. London and New York: Oxford University Press, 1939. (*Synspunktet for min Forfatter-Virksomhed*, by S. Kierkegaard, posthumously published 1859. *Om min Forfatter-Virksomhed*, by S. Kierkegaard, 1851.)

FSE   *For Self-Examination,* trans. Howard V. Hong and Edna
       H. Hong. Minneapolis: Augsburg Publishing House,
       1940. (*Til Selvprovelse,* by S. Kierkegaard, 1851.)

JFY   *Judge for Yourselves!* including *For Self-Examination, Two
       Discourses at the Communion on Fridays* (trans. David
       Swenson) and *The Unchangeableness of God* (trans. Wal-
       ter Lowrie). Princeton: Princeton University Press,
       1944. (*Dommer Selv!* by S. Kierkegaard, 1852; *To Taler
       ved Altergangen om Fredagen,* by S. Kierkegaard, 1851;
       Guds Uforanderlighed, by S. Kierkegaard, 1855.)

KAUC   *Kierkegaard's Attack upon "Christendom,"* 1854-1855,
       trans. Walter Lowrie. Princeton: Princeton University
       Press, 1944. (*Bladartikler* I-XXI, by S. Kierkegaard,
       Fædrelandet, 1954-1955; *Dette skal siges; saa være det da
       sagt,* by S. Kierkegaard, 1955; *Øieblikket,* by S. Kierke-
       gaard, 1-9, 1855; 10, 1905; *Hvad Christus dommer om of-
       ficiel Christendom,* by S. Kierkegaard, 1855.)

JSK   *The Journals of Søren Kierkegaard,* trans. Alexander Dru.
       London and New York: Oxford University Press, 1938.
       (From *Søren Kierkegaards Papirer,* I-XI³ in 18 volumes,
       1909-1936.)

LY   *The Last Years,* trans. Ronald C. Smith. New York:
       Harper and Row, 1965. (From *Papirer XI¹-XI²,* 1936-
       1948.)

JP   *Søren Kierkegaard's Journals and Papers,* trans. Howard
       V. Hong and Edna H. Hong, assisted by Gregor Ma-
       lantschuk. Bloomington and London: Indiana Univer-
       sity Press, 1, 1967; 2, 1970; 3-4, 1975; 5-7, 1978. (From
       Papirer I-XI³ and XII-XIII, 2d ed., and *Breve og Akstykker
       vedrørende Søren Kierkegaard,* ed. Niels Thulstrup, 1-2,
       1953-1954.)

LD   *Letters and Documents,* trans. Hendrik Rosenmeier.
       Princeton: Princeton University Press, 1978.

COR   *The Corsair Affair,* trans. Howard V. Hong and Edna H.
       Hong. Princeton: Princeton University Press, 1982.

A Socratic Introduction

How does one introduce a book about a book—especially if the former is a collection of fresh, new essays and the latter is Kierkegaard's *The Concept of Anxiety?* Is it worthwhile to repeat material that has already appeared as a historical introduction even if one can treat the material argumentatively rather than "objectively?"

Is Professor Dunning simply perverse when he refers to Kierkegaard's *systematic* analysis of anxiety? Can philosophy be "presuppositionless?" Is the notion of a necessary movement logically incoherent? Why could Kierkegaard not have "artfully" presented—with figures, parables, and analogies, or even a novella—the concept of anxiety? Why is this book, perhaps, his most systematic? Given that there is a systematic structure to *The Concept of Anxiety,* what was Kierkegaard's motive in using it?

How is innocence related to anxiety? How does the spirit relate itself to itself? How does the spirit relate itself to externals in the act of self-constitution? to other persons? What possible effect could human sinfulness have upon the nonhuman creation? Is Kierkegaard's distinction between objective and subjective anxiety a viable one? Is the source of sin anxiety or concupiscence? What is the relation of sexuality to anxiety? How is the relation of time and eternity related to anxiety? How can a person, defined as spirit, be characterized as spiritless? How does the concept of anxiety differentiate paganism and Judaism? What is anxiety over evil? over the good? Is the "demonic" a useful concept today? Was it ever? What are the forms of the demonic that Kierkegaard develops? How is faith related to anxiety?

How does Professor Barrett suggest Kierkegaard modified the concepts he inherited from Augustine? from Luther? How polemical is *The Concept of Anxiety* toward the anthropology and theology of G. W. F. Hegel? Can Kierkegaard's position, granted there is only one and that one knows it, be defended from the charge of at least semi-Pelagianism? Why is he so sensitive to Pelagianism? Is Kierkegaard's argument weakened by his lack of knowledge of medieval theology? of orthodox theology? of the Jewish reading of the Scriptures, which does not find in them the heavy-timbered doctrine of hereditary sin so central to the Christian reading of the same Scriptures?

What is "sin" anyway? Is it not possible to be a fully mature, "complete person" without this notion having penetrated one's consciousness? Is hereditary sin a universal phenomenon, appearing in different masks in different religions, or is it, strictly speaking, a Western provincialism? What is the relation of "sin" to "guilt?" Is anything lost in the translation from "original" to "hereditary" sin? Is either term more or less confusing than the other?

Is "sin" a bad decision or is it a corruption of human nature, or is it something else? How is one responsible for "inherited sin," given that it is an intelligible concept? Is hereditary sin an act, a mood, or a state? All three? None of the above? Is Kierkegaard's thought even consistent? What is the relation of the moods to the passions? What is the relation of psychology to hereditary sin? What is the relation of ethics to hereditary sin? Can human understanding comprehend hereditary sin? Is intellectual curiosity a mood proper for understanding hereditary sin? What was "first" about the first sin? How is the first sin qualitatively different from every subsequent sin? How does the notion of original sin unify the race? What is the status of the concept of the human race in Kierkegaard? How is corporate sin related to individual sin? What is the relation of dogmatics to ethics? What is the relation of psychology to dogmatics?

How does Professor Green think Kierkegaard's thought is continuous with that of Kant? how discontinuous? How are Kant's and
Kierkegaard's ideas of freedom similar? how different? How is
Kant's concept of radical evil itself radicalized and modified by
Kierkegaard? Is a divine command heteronomous? How are the
ideality of ethics and the absoluteness of the moral command related to anxiety? Why is sin finally inexplicable in both Kant and
Kierkegaard? Why is the choice of evil inexplicable? How do Kant's
and Kierkegaard's analyses differ? How does Kant's understanding of radical evil distinguish him from the more typical members
of the Enlightenment? Why is repentance the shipwreck of ethics
for both Kant and Kierkegaard?

According to Professor McCarthy, how are Kant, Fichte, Schelling, Hegel, and Kierkegaard related in their understanding of the
origin of sin and the theory of sin's resolution? What is the dialectical tension between Schelling's concept of freedom and Hegel's
concept of necessity? How does Schelling's teaching of the becoming of God relate to Hegel's theory of the becoming of the absolute? Does Hegel have a viable doctrine of potentiality? How does
Schelling attempt to avoid the charge of emanationism and
pantheism? How is evil derived or derivable from God without his
being responsible for it? If God is not responsible for evil, via some
astute reasoning, in spite of its being derived from him, why is man
responsible? Is man accountable while God is not? How does Kierkegaard's concept of the Fall compare and contrast with Schelling's? How does Kierkegaard's concept of "nothing" contrast with
Schelling's *Urgrund* in God? How is Schelling's concept of "heavy-
spiritedness" related to Kierkegaard's concept of anxiety?

Why, Professor Dupré wonders, is Schelling's influence not
made more explicit by Kierkegaard? How can given ideals fail to
jeopardize moral autonomy? How is moral freedom related to a
transcendent absolute? How can man be both free and derived in
some way from an absolute? How does the problem of autonomy
bear on the problems of time and eternity, the synthesizing of time
and eternity by the self to produce itself? How does Kierkegaard's
view of infinity/finitude accept and modify the idealistic philosophy of Hegel? of Schelling? How is infinity a temptation? How is
finitude? How does the subject appropriate the past into present

and future projects? Why is the future a particular problem in self-actualization?

Why does Professor Roberts think that atheism was inconceivable to Kierkegaard? How broad is the God-relationship in Kierkegaard? Is a "pagan" knowledge of God, that is, a natural knowledge of God, possible? How is the natural knowledge of God related to self-knowledge? How deeply does the Socratic sense of self-knowledge inform Kierkegaard's view of the possibility of a natural knowledge of God? To what extent is anxiety a construct of reality? To what extent is anxiety a variant in a person's makeup? Does this variation in any way reflect on the universal claims of the Christian gospel? What has anxiety to do with possibility? How does anxiety beget the God-relationship? Why does determinism suffocate the God-relation, moral responsibility, and the self? In self-knowledge, does one experience God's presence, or does one come to realize the need for God and in that context postulate God as an object of belief? Can there be an experience of God apart from some minimal concept of God? Is it not rather presumptuous of man to think he is the object of a divine concern? Is the final issue nothingness or the divine?

Is the life of faith, Professor Hall queries, compatible with a theory of community? Does the inescapability of language refute the charge that Kierkegaard's individualism forecloses the possibility of community in his thought? Can the demonically shut-up life come to openness, to expression, to community, according to Kierkegaard? Is shut-upness a characteristic of the demonic or of the religious, according to Kierkegaard? What is anxiety about the good? How is freedom related to the good? How does authentic or existential speech, the use of words one has earned the right to use, bear on the issue of community in Kierkegaard's thought? What is the difference between "being able to be silent" and shut-upness?

Why did Heidegger not treat Kierkegaard as a philosophical writer concerned with being, according to Professor Magurshak? How does Heidegger go beyond Kierkegaard's "existentiell" account of human existence to an "existential" one? Is the distinction itself valid? Is Heidegger's critique of Kierkegaard justified? Is there a perspective from which both Heidegger's and Kierkegaard's projects can be critically viewed and interpreted? What are the major differences between the projects of Heidegger and Kierkegaard? Is it possible to secularize Kierkegaard's ontic "deliberations on the dogmatic issue of hereditary sin" in order to develop a true, though nontheological, view of human being? Why did Heidegger undertake the analysis of *Dasein* and what did Kierkegaard's analysis of anxiety contribute to that task? Why is anxiety necessary to the achievement of human wholeness, authenticity? What is the difference between Kierkegaard's and Heidegger's concepts of "nothingness?" Did Heidegger appreciate or even understand Kierkegaard's concept of time? How is "inauthenticity" related to Kierkegaard's interpretation of aesthetic existence? What do both Kierkegaard and Heidegger owe to the Socratic concept of self-knowledge? What are the differences between Kierkegaard's and Heidegger's analyses of being human?

Is this the end of the matter?

Robert L. Perkins

I

Kierkegaard's Systematic Analysis of Anxiety

by Stephen N. Dunning

That the True is actual only as system, or that Substance is essentially Subject, is expressed in the representation of the Absolute as *Spirit*—the most sublime Notion and the one which belongs to the modern age and its religion. The spiritual alone is the *actual*; it is essence, or that which has *being in itself*; it is that which *relates itself to itself* and is *determinate,* it is *other-being* and *being-for-self,* and in this determinateness, or in its self-externality, abides within itself; in other words, it is *in and for itself.*

G. W. F. Hegel[1]

The subjective thinker has a form, a form for his communication with other men, and this form constitutes his style. It must be as manifold as the opposites he holds in combination. The systematic *ein, zwei, drei* is an abstract form, and must therefore fail when applied to the concrete. In

---

[1]G. W. F. Hegel, *Phenomenology of Spirit,* trans. A. V. Miller (Oxford: Clarendon Press, 1977) 14.

the same degree as the subjective thinker himself is concrete, his form will become concretely dialectical.

S. Kierkegaard[2]

The issue appears to be clear. According to Hegel, actuality can be understood only in systematic terms, terms involving three dialectical moments: an in-itself moment in which a phenomenon appears as an immediate unity; a for-itself moment in which the immediacy and unity are sundered as the phenomenon appears in a form contradictory to the first moment; and an in-and-for-itself moment in which the phenomenon is reconciled with itself, internalizing its own "other-being" and abiding with itself again, not in an immediate or simple unity but as a complex and internally differentiated whole that takes up into itself both of the previous moments. This "taking up" is the famous Hegelian *Aufhebung*, a concept Hegel uses to express the idea that the first two moments perish as mere contradictions but are preserved in their true relation within the third.[3]

Kierkegaard is unrestrained in his ridicule of such philosophical mumbo jumbo. His attacks on Hegel's claims for "necessity" and a "presuppositionless" beginning are well known and may or may not be based upon an adequate understanding of Hegel—the question of "misreading" looms large.[4] But, as the passage quoted

---

[2]CUP, 319. I have used the third Danish edition of Kierkegaard's *Samlede Vaerker* (hereinafter cited as SV), ed. A. B. Drachman, J. L. Heiberg, and H. O. Lange (Copenhagen: Gyldendal, 1963), which I cite in footnotes wherever I have found it necessary to revise the English translation.

[3]Many possible translations of *Aufhebung* have been suggested: sublation, sublimation, abrogation, transformation, overcoming, and annulment are but a few examples. None, however, carries the peculiar double meaning of the German that Hegel so persistently exploits.

[4]See Harold Bloom, *A Map of Misreading* (Oxford: Oxford University Press, 1975).

above demonstrates, he also attacks Hegel's belief in the systematic nature of actuality. In Kierkegaard's view, the triadic dialectic so revered by Hegel is nothing but an abstract form, utterly inadequate for explaining the concreteness of reality. A truly dialectical analysis must be concrete rather than abstractly systematic.

The irony is that Kierkegaard is unable to avoid those very systematic structures that he so constantly disparages in Hegel's writings. However much he may reject systematic thinking, a number of his major pseudonymous works are susceptible to analysis in terms of progressive triads (in-itself, for-itself, in-and-for-itself) of conceptual development.[5] Nowhere is this susceptibility more apparent than in *The Concept of Anxiety*, a work that manifests not merely occasional Hegelian elements but a clear and coherent systematic structure from start to finish.[6] This structure does not, however, coincide with the organization of the text to a degree sufficient to show that Kierkegaard himself consciously intends it. Although bits and pieces of it may be inserted as irony or even parody, there is no reason to explain the entire structure in this way. On

---

[5]A striking example is the dialectic of aesthetic immediacy in *Either/Or* 1. My analysis of the structure of the essays in that volume can be found in "The Dialectic of Contradiction in Kierkegaard's Aesthetic Stage," *Journal of the American Academy of Religion* 49, no. 3 (September 1981): 383-408.

[6]Vincent A. McCarthy explores some of the Hegelian elements in " 'Psychological Fragments': Kierkegaard's Religious Psychology," in *Kierkegaard's Truth: The Disclosure of the Self*, vol. 5 of *Psychiatry and the Humanities*, ed. Joseph H. Smith (New Haven: Yale University Press, 1981) 253. See also in the same volume Paul Ricoeur's "Two Encounters with Kierkegaard: Kierkegaard and Evil and Doing Philosophy after Kierkegaard," 313-42. Kresten Nordentoft observes that some passages in *The Concept of Anxiety* are "almost word-for-word identical with some introductory observations in a book to which he himself refers later in *The Concept of Anxiety*, namely, the German philosopher Karl Rosenkranz' *Psychologie*. The similarity does not mean that Kierkegaard is simply plagiarizing this German pupil of Hegel, but it shows that Kierkegaard is taking his point of origin in views which were well-known in his time, while he continues his analysis in a completely original way" (*Kierkegaard's Psychology*, trans. Bruce Kirmmse [Pittsburgh: Duquesne University Press, 1978] 21). *The Concept of Anxiety* also resembles Rosenkranz's work in that they both have systematically dialectical structures, obvious and intentional in the latter, but obscure in the former. Although there are occasional parallels within those structures, Nordentoft's point about Kierkegaard's originality is well taken. See Karl Rosenkranz, *Psychologie, oder die Wissenschaft vom subjectiven Geist* (Königsberg: Bornträger, 1837).

the contrary, the more likely conjecture is that Kierkegaard was unaware of the extent to which he continued, even after breaking with Hegelian thought, to think in patterns that conformed to Hegelian systematic structures.

This essay is primarily a demonstration that there is a similar structure in *The Concept of Anxiety*.[7] Such a demonstration requires an unusual amount of summarizing and analyzing of the text, since my argument is based entirely upon the correspondence between the text as it stands and the structure I discern in it. This is a particularly difficult task for what has justly been called "possibly the most difficult of Kierkegaard's works."[8] In addition to showing that the structure is there, my analysis will make two other contributions to scholarly interpretation of this book. One is an argument showing that *The Concept of Anxiety* is best understood as dealing with the religious stage of existence, for it is very much a treatise on the problem of sin, and Kierkegaard always associated sin-consciousness with the religious stage.[9] The other point concerns the

---

[7]In my book, *Kierkegaard's Dialectic of Inwardness* (forthcoming from Princeton University Press), this type of analysis is expanded to include the entire theory of stages.

[8]Reidar Thomte in his historical introduction (CA, xii).

[9]*The Concept of Anxiety* is almost like a mirror, reflecting to each interpreter what interests that interpreter most. It is certainly one of the best examples of those dialectical structures that so fascinate me. Josiah Thompson, with his psychobiographical approach, reads it as a statement about Kierkegaard's personal experiences of anxiety and despair (*The Lonely Labyrinth: Kierkegaard's Pseudonymous Works* [Carbondale: Southern Illinois University Press, 1967] 150-64), and appropriately deals with it while discussing the aesthetic stage (see also "The Master of Irony," in *Kierkegaard: A Collection of Critical Essays*, ed. Josiah Thompson [Garden City: Doubleday Anchor, 1972] 127-29). Vincent McCarthy also places it in the aesthetic, due to Haufniensis's emphasis upon withdrawnness and the demonic, although the latter category seems to me to be primarily religious (see *The Phenomenology of Moods in Kierkegaard* [The Hague: Martinus Nijhoff, 1978] 45, 52). Mark C. Taylor's fascination with the process of decision by which the self moves into the ethical stage and then goes on to Christianity leads him to include *The Concept of Anxiety* in his treatments of both the ethical and the religious stages (*Kierkegaard's Pseudonymous Authorship: A Study of Time and the Self* [Princeton: Princeton University Press, 1975] 217ff., 269ff.). My claim that it belongs primarily to the religious is based upon my analysis in this essay, although I happily cite a supporting remark by Johannes Climacus: "anxiety represents [the individual's] state of mind in the desperate emancipation from the task of realizing the ethical" (CUP, 240; SV, 9:225).

status of the eternal in *The Concept of Anxiety*. According to some scholars, it remains external to the human subject throughout the book.[10] Structural analysis shows, to the contrary, that one of the most important accomplishments of the dialectical development of anxiety is precisely the internalization of the eternal. In this work, the dialectics of inner/outer and self/other, which are so prominent throughout the pseudonymous authorship, are united in one of Kierkegaard's most significant characterizations of the divine, namely, the concept of the eternal as an other that can be known only inwardly.

The pseudonymous author of *The Concept of Anxiety* is Vigilius Haufniensis, which means "watchman of Copenhagen." He introduces himself in the preface as a "layman who indeed speculates but is still far removed from speculation," presumably because speculation requires a rejection of all positive authorities, and Haufniensis has no desire to do that (CA, 8). Indeed, the purpose of the introduction, which is a very involved discussion of the relation of psychology to ethics and dogmatics, is really to locate those disciplines and their various understandings of sin in relation to the question of authority. After criticizing Hegel for attempting to synthesize the realms of possibility (abstract thought) and actuality (existence) by means of mediation, Haufniensis characterizes the differences among the various approaches to sin.

It is worth summarizing what he says about each discipline in turn (CA, 20-24). The "first ethics" is a pagan science that ignores sin and is "shipwrecked on the sinfulness of the single individual." This pagan ethics assumes the goodness of human nature and then cannot account for the actual sin that characterizes human behavior in history. Psychology explores the real possibility of sin, but ignores sin's actuality; it comes no closer than the "restless repose" out of which "sin constantly arises." It is in dogmatics that hereditary sin as sin's "ideal possibility" is explained, thus providing the foundation for "the second ethics," which Haufniensis calls

---

[10]Gregor Malantschuk writes that Haufniensis treats "the eternal *outside of man*," but ignores "the eternal *in man*." See *Kierkegaard's Thought*, ed. and trans. Howard V. Hong and Edna H. Hong (Princeton: Princeton University Press, 1971) 340. The italics are Malantschuk's. McCarthy agrees in *Moods*, 89.

the "new science." This is clearly Christian ethics, which is interested not in the possibility of sin or even in hereditary sin but only in the actuality of sin—the fact that human life is under the sway of sin. *The Concept of Anxiety* is presented as a psychological treatment of the dogmatic problem of hereditary sin, although in later chapters it also deals with "the second ethics," or the consciousness of sin as an actuality.

The first two chapters, however, are psychological in the sense stated above: they attempt to explain the real possibility of hereditary sin by appealing to the concept of anxiety.[11] In chapter 1, anxiety is said to explain hereditary sin "retrogressively in terms of its origin"; in chapter 2, it does so "progressively" in terms of its consequences. In both of these chapters, then, there is an abstract positing of anxiety as the possibility of sin. Sin and anxiety are posited in general, not in relation to the experience of individuals. Without ever claiming that his analysis is systematically dialectical, Haufniensis opens his essay with the notion of abstract anxiety "in-itself."

Chapter 1 deals with the question "How could sin have entered the world?" One traditional method is to pin the blame on Adam, to interpret the Genesis story as the passing from innocence to guilt through Adam and Eve, and then to attribute the sin and guilt of all subsequent generations to their first sin. This will not do, argues Haufniensis in article 1, for it places Adam "fantastically" outside of history, and thus begs the question. If Adam is as different from historical human beings as this interpretation implies, then his first sin is not really a human event; by implica-

---

[11]A note on the translation of *Angest* (German, *Angst*): Walter Lowrie confesses the impossibility of finding an English word that captures both the present painfulness (anguish) and the orientation toward the future (dread) that are implied in Kierkegaard's use of this word. See his preface to Søren Kierkegaard, *The Concept of Dread*, trans. Walter Lowrie (Princeton: Princeton University Press, 1957) x. He settles on "dread," a decision that some leading contemporary scholars still support (e.g., Taylor, *Authorship*, 219n.). However, the consensus now is to use "anxiety," which reduces the intensity of the pain but preserves the future orientation (see, e.g., the glossary to Kierkegaard's *The Concept of Irony*, 432). This is Howard Hong's decision for the new English edition, *Kierkegaard's Writings* (thus Thomte in *The Concept of Anxiety*), and I shall follow it, more to avoid confusion than out of conviction that "anxiety" is preferable to "dread."

tion, it is almost shoved back into the creation event itself, which renders it fantastic or mythical. No, Adam's sin must be essentially *human* sin, so that whatever explains the sin of one explains the sin of all.

Article 2 develops the relation between Adam, the first sinner, and other sinners by distinguishing between sin and sinfulness. Whereas sin enters the world identically in each individual, so that Adam is not to be blamed for any other person's sin, sinfulness entered the world with Adam's sin, and therefore cannot be said to have "entered" again. Sin is a *qualitative* leap from innocence to guilt that can occur only by an actual sin. Sinfulness is a *quantitative* designation of the disposition to sin. Sin is a dialectical contradiction in that it presupposes itself. Sinfulness is the psychological/ethical characteristic that results from sin.

The third and fourth articles elaborate upon what has already been established. Since sin entered the world by a leap, a dialectical contradiction, it is a wrong to say that innocence is "annulled," as Hegel does when he identifies innocence with immediacy. Haufniensis accuses Hegel of a category error, for immediacy, as a category of logic, has nothing to do with existence. Innocence is ignorance, a state of existence that is "annulled only by guilt." And the leap into guilt defies explanation; psychology can at best explain the conditions for the Fall, not the Fall itself.

This discussion brings Haufniensis to the concept of anxiety (article 5). Interpreters often seize upon his paradoxical formulation of anxiety as *"a sympathetic antipathy and an antipathetic sympathy"* (CA, 42) as the essence of anxiety, but that phrase is intelligible only in terms of the discussion of otherness that constitutes its context. Haufniensis states that innocence is a striving against nothing, and that this nothing "begets anxiety." Furthermore, "innocence always sees this nothing outside itself." That thought is developed in the following paragraph, in which innocent anxiety is defined as "a determination of dreaming spirit,"[12]

---

[12]CA, 41; SV, 6:136. I have employed "determination" for *Bestemmelse* throughout this essay, since it, rather than "qualification," is the normal equivalent for *Bestimmung* in works by Hegel. The dialectical parallel here between dreaming anxiety and dreaming desire (in EO, 1:74-77, 83) is unmistakable.

and dreaming is compared with other states of consciousness in terms of how each perceives the other: awake, one is conscious of the other as other; asleep, the difference between self and other is suspended; and when dreaming, the other is "an intimated nothing." In short, if innocence is the spirit while dreaming, and dreaming consciousness perceives the other as nothing, then one can conclude that the "nothing" that begets anxiety is in fact the dreaming consciousness of an *undetermined other*. This is confirmed later in the article when Haufniensis asks, "How does spirit relate itself to itself and to its conditionality? It relates itself as anxiety. Do away with itself, the spirit cannot; lay hold of itself, it cannot, as long as it has itself outside of itself" (CA, 44).

From these passages, it is reasonable to conclude that the key to the anxiety of innocence is that the self is looking for itself in others, in externals, outside of itself, but without focusing on specific others. Thus, its other is a nothing, which in turn helps to explain the paradox of sympathetic antipathy and antipathetic sympathy. The other that is nothing both attracts and repels the innocent spirit, which both hopes and fears that it might lay hold of itself in the other, thereby finding and losing itself simultaneously. This paradox illuminates several other formulations of the anxiety of innocence: it is "pleasing anxiety"; it is "freedom's actuality as the possibility of possibility," namely, the actuality here is an other that is also a nothing and is thus only the possibility of possibility; and "the less spirit, the less anxiety" (CA, 42), for spirit is the quest for selfhood, a quest that begets anxiety with its initial insight that the self is—a nothing.

In the course of the fifth article, Haufniensis defines man as a synthesis in the spirit of the psychical and the physical. He utilizes this definition in the sixth and final article to distinguish between sin and sexuality. The fall into sin occurs in the spirit. Thus, it affects both the soul and the body, for they are united in the spirit. By virtue of sin, bodily sensuousness becomes sexuality, for "without sin there is no sexuality" (CA, 49). Simultaneously, with sin the soul becomes sinful. Thus, sinfulness is not to be equated with sensuousness or even with sexuality, although psychical sinfulness and physical sexuality are the sibling offspring of sin.

With sexuality, history begins, and this beginning raises again the question of freedom. Haufniensis denies the necessity of the Fall (for its necessity would be a contradiction and would eliminate anxiety) and also the notion of a voluntary Fall by a totally free will, which he dismisses as "a nuisance for thought." Instead, he suggests that anxiety is "entangled freedom, where freedom is not free in itself but entangled, not by necessity, but in itself" (CA, 49). Once again, the implication is that of a leap: sin comes into the world by a sin, and there is no one else to blame for one's guilt but oneself. Sin is not mediated to the sinner by any means whatsoever: it is "that transcendence, that *descrimen rerum* [crisis] in which sin enters into the single individual as the single individual" (CA, 50).

But it is not yet time to consider sin and anxiety in relation to the individual. Haufniensis has offered his interpretation of anxiety as the presupposition or origin of hereditary sin, and this interpretation has led him to consider the problems of sensuousness and of history. In chapter 2, he deals with these together under the rubric of generation. Generation embraces the double meaning of sexual reproduction and development through time, and so it focuses very nicely the issue that Haufniensis wishes to explore, namely, anxiety as the consequence of hereditary sin, as that which explains hereditary sin progressively. He believes that, although a more primitive person has more profound anxiety, in fact "hereditary sin is growing" (CA, 52).

The two areas in which sin and sinfulness produce anxiety give the chapter its structure. One is the natural world, the "eager longing" of creation mentioned in Romans 8:19, which Haufniensis calls objective anxiety. The other is the self's subjective anxiety prior to positing itself as guilty of sin.

Objective anxiety is the "effect of sin in nonhuman existence (*Tilvaerelse*)" (CA, 57). It is not that inanimate objects are to be regarded as sinful, but that "creation is placed in an entirely different light because of Adam's sin," for now "sensuousness is constantly degraded to mean sinfulness" (CA, 58). This statement shows that what is really at stake here is the perception of creation by sinful humans.[13] Because of the fact of sin, the distinction be-

---

[13]It is the same with "the irony of nature." See CI, 271n.

tween sensuousness (sinless bodily existence) and sinfulness (the psychical result of sin) is blurred. This is tantamount to saying that sinfulness is projected onto sensuousness. In the same way, the external created world seems to manifest an objective anxiety. This anxiety is, by virtue of its innocence or lack of self-consciousness, analogous to (although less than) that of Adam (CA, 60).

Subjective anxiety is also analogous to the anxiety of Adam, although it is quantitatively greater by virtue of generation. Haufniensis is saying that the relationship of generation is "the something that the nothing of anxiety may signify in the subsequent individual" (CA, 62). That is, generation refers to the subsequent individual's search for self in the other, in that which is external. Hence, the bulk of this section on subjective anxiety is devoted to what at first appear to be two digressions—one on the relationship between generation and woman (CA, 63-67) and the other on sexuality (CA, 67-72). When Haufniensis announces, "We shall now return to the subject with which we were dealing, namely, the consequence of the relationship of generation in the individual" (CA, 72), one is tempted to ask what the preceding ten pages accomplished. For the main point with regard to generation is adequately made by his emphasized remark: "*anxiety about sin produces sin*" (CA, 73). Born into a sinful world, the individual becomes anxious about the possibility of sin, and this anxiety, rather than any innate concupiscence, is what results in sin; even anxiety about being thought guilty can lead to guilt (CA, 75).

Once again, it is the dialectic of self and other that can provide a fuller grasp of Haufniensis's argument. For that understanding it is necessary to return to those apparent digressions on generation in relation to woman and to sexuality. The first recalls the synthesis of the psychical and the physical, for Haufniensis claims that there will be more anxiety whenever that synthesis is "cleft" by an imbalance in the two parts. Since woman is more sensuous than man, he reasons, she must also have more anxiety (CA, 64). The consideration of woman leads to a discussion of the medium of the male-female relationship (namely, sexuality), which confirms that the origin of anxiety is the search for self in another self.

Haufniensis's analysis of the erotic has a dialectical structure of its own. First he discusses the "sexual as such," which he says is not sinful. Since only beasts are genuinely ignorant of sexuality, human innocence must be understood as "a knowledge . . . that has ignorance as its first determination."[14] He suggests calling this state modesty, for it manifests the anxiety of shame, if not yet the anxiety of lust. In other words, the awareness of the other as other is just beginning to appear in sexuality as such: "In modesty, the generic difference is posited, but not in relation to its other. That relation takes place in the sexual drive" (CA, 69), which is not only instinct but also propagation. Propagation is not yet love. Indeed, from the point of view of paganism, it appears comic, which leads Haufniensis to comment that the "anxiety in modesty arose from the spirit's feeling that it was a foreigner; now spirit has conquered completely and perceives the sexual as the foreign and as the comic" (CA, 69). Thus, the erotic is conquered by propagation, by means of its relationship to its other; whereas modesty remains afraid of the erotic and sexually inhibited by its lack of such a relationship. In Christianity, the self discovers that "the religious has suspended the erotic . . . because in spirit there is no difference between man and woman" (CA, 70). In other words, the distinction between self and other that sexuality has brought about is also sublated in the spirit—but at the price of the erotic. Because the erotic is suspended and spirit is excluded from it, there is still anxiety, for anxiety occurs whenever the spirit "feels itself a stranger" (CA, 71). Even if the sexual is brought fully "under the determination of the spirit," the result is "the victory of love" in which "the sexual is forgotten, and recollected only in forgetfulness. When this has come about, sensuousness is transfigured in spirit and anxiety is driven out."[15]

This analysis of the first two chapters of *The Concept of Anxiety* has yielded two significant results. First, it has shown that anxiety is a matter of the dialectic of self and other. It originates when the self seeks itself in an other, and it can be characterized as the state of a self that is other ("a stranger") to itself. Anxiety is the root and

---

[14]CA, 68; SV, 6:159.

[15]CA, 80; SV, 6:169. On the identity of male and female in Christianity, see Galatians 3:28.

result of alienation, understood as a distorted relationship to one-self and to others. Second, this analysis has shown this concept of anxiety to be susceptible to a systematic, structural analysis. As a mere concept, it is the movement of anxiety in-itself. This first movement simply posits anxiety as the theoretical origin and re-sult of hereditary sin. Actual sin is not yet distinguished from the hereditary condition of sinfulness; nor is there as yet any con-sciousness of sin.

Within this movement, three moments can be discerned.[16] In the first, the self seeks itself in an indeterminate other. This is dreaming anxiety, the in-itself moment in which self and other have not yet been distinguished at all. It is followed by objective anxi-ety, a for-itself moment in which the self projects its anxiety onto creation, which is the nonhuman other.[17] Here, self and other are distinguished, but in a very unsatisfactory way, for the self re-mains unaware of its own anxiety. That consciousness appears only in the in-and-for-itself moment, which Haufniensis labels subjec-tive anxiety. Here the self finds itself in a human other, which is a good deal closer to its actual self than either the indeterminate or the nonhuman other. Within subjective anxiety, the self finds it-self by means of a dialectic of erotic relations. Modesty is the in-itself phase, in which the self is aware of sexual difference but not yet in relation to a particular other. That relationship first appears as propagation, a for-itself phase in which the opposition between the spirit and sexuality becomes explicit. Whereas spirit feels alien-ated in modesty, now it is sexuality that is alienated from the self by virtue of being harnessed and subjected to the goal of propa-gation. This dialectical struggle between modesty and propaga-tion illustrates that the erotic is not yet spirit, for they both are phases in which the self is still seeking itself in an other. The the-

---

[16]In an effort to minimize confusion, I employ "movement" for the most ab-stract structural level, "moment" for the middle, and "phase" for the most con-crete. Thus, *The Concept of Anxiety* includes three movements, each of which has three moments, and some of those moments have an internal development of three phases.

[17]I disagree with McCarthy, who suggests that the section on objective anxiety is included merely "for form's sake" and therefore seems "a bit forced" (*Moods*, 40-41).

oretical resolution of this contradiction is posited by Christianity, which asserts the self's identity with its other. With this new consciousness, the movement of abstract anxiety—that is, anxiety projected onto something or someone other—is complete. The self understands that its anxiety is about itself, and the for-itself movement of anxiety can begin.

Chapter 3 presents anxiety as a consciousness of the eternal that is not yet conscious of hereditary sin, in short, a consciousness that is religious without being Christian. It is here that Haufniensis dialectically situates Christian paganism, paganism, and Judaism in relation to each other and to Christianity.[18] The fundamental dialectic is no longer that of psyche and body; it is the eternal and the temporal. "In the individual life," he begins, "anxiety is the Moment" (CA, 81).[19] This is neither a dialectical moment nor a temporal instant. On the contrary, the intention of Haufniensis's discussion is to refute the Hegelian theory that eternity is the totality and infinite succession of temporal moments.

The Moment occurs, writes Haufniensis, when "time and eternity touch each other . . . in time." He praises the Danish word *Øiblikket* (which, like the German *Augenblick*, means "blink of the eye") as a "beautiful word" (CA, 87). This touching-in-time of eternity and time is not in any sense a mediation of equal poles: "the Moment is not properly an atom of time but an atom of eternity. It is the first reflection of eternity in time, its first attempt, as it were, at stopping time" (CA, 88). Eternity, then, is that which attempts to stop time. Rather than an infinite extension of time, it breaks into time from the outside and limits it. This limitation, this instant in which the limit of time is revealed, is the Moment.

On the basis of this understanding of the Moment, it is possible to grasp Haufniensis's concept of temporality. Temporality is posited on the basis of the Moment, and history begins with it. In short,

---

[18]This is obviously not a historical progression, or Christian paganism could not precede paganism and Judaism. Gregor Malantschuk nonetheless implies that it might be (*Kierkegaard's Way to the Truth,* trans. Mary Michelsen [Minneapolis: Augsburg, 1963] ch. 2; see also *Thought,* 265-66).

[19]In order to distinguish the Moment when eternity enters time from both dialectical moments and moments in a temporal series, I shall capitalize it.

although the Moment occurs in the blink of an eye, it brings about a qualitative change within the temporal sequence. In the ordinary view, the past, present, and future spill into one another, for future time becomes present and then past in turn. The distinctions between them are merely relative to the particular point of view, which, in itself, is without absolute significance. But if the Moment is the limitation of time by eternity, then temporality is seen as a relation to that time-stopping eternity, not simply to infinite succession. Furthermore, the Moment when eternity breaks into time is not relative to the totality of time; on the contrary, the eternal relativizes time itself and thereby determines the condition of temporality. The distinction of past, present, and future now takes on real significance, for they are each understood in relation to the eternal-in-time, the Moment, rather than in a "simple continuity." That is what is meant by the Christian concept of the "fullness of time" (CA, 90). However, it is true that temporality suffers the same consequence of the positing of sin that sensuousness does: it comes to signify sinfulness (CA, 93).

The dialectic of anxiety in the individual life is structured according to the distinction made by the Moment between present, future, and past. There are three moments, each reflecting a new consciousness of the Moment. The first such moment is Christian paganism, which "really knows no distinction between the present, the past, the future, and the eternal" (CA, 94). Haufniensis labels this "the anxiety of spiritlessness" (article 1). The dilemma of spiritlessness is that, on the one hand, it shares in the Christian relation to spirit; and, on the other, it represses its consciousness of this relation by affecting a pagan indifference to the eternal in time. However, paganism should not be confused with spiritlessness: "the former is qualified *toward* spirit and the latter *away from* spirit" (CA, 95). Since spiritlessness excludes spirit, it also excludes consciousness of anxiety. But anxiety is waiting and will appear as a "profound terror" at the moment of death (CA, 96).

Article 2 bears the title "Anxiety Defined Dialectically as Fate" and deals with paganism as such. Here spirit is no longer excluded, for fate is "a relation to spirit as external" (CA, 96). In other words, the pagan submits to fate as it is revealed through external and accidental means (for example, the oracle, which may be based upon interpreting the entrails of an animal or upon anatomical patterns). Because of this dependence upon such ambiguous and external elements, it is impossible for the pagan to arrive at the concepts of guilt and sin, which presuppose an inward relationship to the eternal. Indeed, it is a meaningless contradiction to affirm that one becomes guilty by fate (CA, 97). Haufniensis develops the pagan position in a long discussion of genius, a discussion that is particularly interesting due to his use of the inner/outer categories. The genius manifests a significant contradiction between a pagan external dependency upon some "insignificance" through which personal fate is revealed and the fact that, for him, the "outward as such has no significance. . . . Everything depends upon how he himself understands it in the presence of his secret friend (fate)" (CA, 100).

The final dialectical moment of anxiety in relation to the eternal in time is guilt (article 3). The historical subject here is Judaism. An important distinction is made immediately: Jewish anxiety is over the possibility of guilt, not the actual consciousness of guilt, which would abolish anxiety with repentance. The anxiety that characterizes Judaism is more advanced than that of Greek culture, since guilt is more inward than fate, but it still manifests a capitulation to externality. According to Haufniensis, "the profound tragedy of Judaism, analogous to the relation of the oracle in paganism," is its dependence upon sacrificial rituals. That rituals increase rather than relieve anxiety about guilt is demonstrated by the necessity of their being constantly repeated (the same is true in a qualified sense, adds Haufniensis, of Catholicism) (CA, 103-104).

The remainder of this chapter on anxiety over the possibility of actual sin (anxiety for-itself) deals with the relation of religious inwardness to external expression: "to explain how my religious existence comes into relation with and expresses itself in my outward existence, that is the task" (CA, 105). The connection between inwardness and guilt is argued by Haufniensis on the basis of Jewish ceremonial law: "In turning toward himself, he [the religious genius] *eo ipso* turns toward God, and there is a ceremonial rule that says that when the finite spirit would see God, it must begin as guilty. As he turns toward himself, he discovers guilt. The greater the genius, the more profoundly he discovers guilt" (CA, 107).

Thus, guilt is the inevitable result of the inward turn, since the turn inward is, by its very nature, a turn toward God. In a comment that shows the extent to which Haufniensis is oblivious to the complex systematic structure within his own analysis, he adds that guilt is the *Ansich* or in-itself of freedom (CA, 108). Although he does not develop this dialectical terminology at all, it is likely that he has in mind a dialectic of anxiety as entangled freedom (CA, 49) in which the three moments are guilt, sin-consciousness, and faith.

To summarize the development of the dialectic of anxiety thus far: in anxiety in-itself, anxiety is not yet self-conscious. It can apprehend itself only through self-projection onto nonhuman and human others. Once the self realizes that the other about which it is anxious is really identical with itself, it advances to anxiety as a condition of the individual life. This is anxiety-for-itself, and Haufniensis traces its three historical expressions, all of which reveal that the self has not yet abandoned the search for itself (now, the eternal) in something external. The continuity between the first two movements can be stated as follows: in anxiety in-itself, the self seeks itself in another that is external; in anxiety for-itself, the self turns to something external in search of the eternal, which is really the Moment or the divine other.

The internal development of anxiety for-itself follows the familiar pattern: the first moment is Christendom,[20] a state in which the consciousness of the eternal has been repressed and with it consciousness of anxiety over the need for the eternal. Anxiety must, in such a person, wait for the fear of death, which will certainly stimulate such a sense of need. The pagan does not repress the need for the eternal, but seeks it externally. Thus, the pagan lives in anxious self-contradiction: the inner need for and relation with the eternal as one's own fate is acknowledged, but the knowledge of that fate is available only externally, in the ambiguous or-

---

[20]The use of "Christendom" here for what Haufniensis calls Christian paganism is justified insofar as both refer to a situation where Christianity has been abandoned in substance but not in name. Of course, Kierkegaard develops a rich and complex critique of Christendom in his later writings, which is adumbrated but not encompassed by this section of *The Concept of Anxiety*.

acle. Judaism overcomes the opposition between Christendom and paganism in that it internalizes the cause of alienation of the self from the eternal. By positing the possibility of guilt, Judaism admits anxiety (with paganism) but focuses that anxiety on the self (as Christendom focuses on the self in indifference to the eternal). But, in attempting to atone for guilt by the performance of rituals, Judaism seeks an external reconciliation with the eternal, an outward solution to an inner problem. This effort is doomed to failure, for, as the Jew has already discovered, freedom is to be discovered only by "turning inward" (CA, 108), since guilt "never has an external occasion, and whoever yields to temptation is himself guilty of the temptation" (CA, 109).

In chapter 4 anxiety as the consequence or consciousness of sin in the single individual at last appears. Haufniensis stresses that this appearance cannot be reduced to a causal chain. Like freedom, sin must never be understood as in any sense necessary, for then the freedom would be unfree and the sin would not be sinful: "the circle of the leap [would be made] into a straight line" (CA, 112). Nevertheless, there is a clear dialectical transition from anxiety for-itself to this final movement, anxiety in-and-for-itself.

The simplest way to express this transition is in terms of the relation of inwardness to externality. In the first movement, there is a dialectic of self and other but no distinction between the temporal and the eternal. That distinction takes place in anxiety for-itself, where the temporal self is determined by its external relations to the eternal. In this third movement, the eternal appears inwardly, in the self's relation to itself. Although this appearance of "the eternal in man" (CA, 151) is not explicit until the second moment, it is implicit in the first moment, anxiety about evil.

Another striking development at this point, and the one that Haufniensis himself emphasizes, is the development from anxiety about the possibility of actual sin to anxiety about actual sin. For the first time, "the object of anxiety is a determinate something and its nothing is an actual something" (CA, 111). Here the indeterminateness of Judaism comes to an end: the individual is a sinner.

Sin is posited as "an annulled possibility," that is, as an actuality.[21] The question is no longer whether one is in sin, but what, if anything, can be done about it.

That consciousness would like to do something about it is immediately clear from the passage with which article 1 ("Anxiety about Evil") opens: "The posited sin is indeed an annulled possibility, but it is also an unwarranted actuality, and as such, anxiety can relate itself to it. Since sin is an unwarranted actuality, it is also to be negated. This work anxiety will undertake" (CA, 113). It appears that the very realization of sin as a fact brings with it the hope—and anxiety—of becoming free from it. Thus, this first moment begins with "the ingenious sophistry of anxiety," for the actuality of sin immediately proclaims freedom, on the one hand, and "the eloquence of illusion" on the other (CA, 113). This phase is followed by a second, in which anxiety sees the possibility of the continuation of sin and tries to strike a compromise with it: anxiety "wants to have the actuality of sin continue—but note, only to a certain degree" (CA, 114). The sophistry of anxiety and the impotence of compromise are united in repentance, which both hopes for freedom and impotently confesses sin: "Repentance is reduced to a possibility in relation to sin; in other words, repentance cannot cancel sin, it can only sorrow over it."[22] The repentant self has no strength on which to draw. Conquered by sin, the anxiety of the individual "throws itself despairingly into the arms of repentance" (CA, 115), which Haufniensis implicitly compares with death.

> The only thing that is truly able to disarm the sophistry of sin is faith, courage to believe that the state itself is a new sin, courage to renounce anxiety without anxiety, which only faith can do; faith does not thereby annihilate anxiety, but, itself eternally young, it extricates itself from anxiety's moment of death. Only faith is able

---

[21]The Danish for this bit of technical Hegelian jargon is *en ophævet Mulighed* (CA, 113; SV, 6:198). From a comment by Johannes Climacus about guilt-consciousness (CUP, 474; SV, 10:205), it is clear that this is an actuality in which the development is from abstract to concrete. See also the editor's note to that passage, SV, 10:303. For another systematically dialectical analysis of guilt and sin, one in which their order is reversed, see Paul Ricoeur, *The Symbolism of Evil*, trans. Emerson Buchanan (Boston: Beacon Press, 1969) 47-150.

[22]CA, 115; SV, 6:199. The Danish word that translates *cancel* is *hæve*.

to do this, for only in faith is the synthesis eternal and at every moment possible (CA, 117).

The synthesis referred to has many applications—physical and psychical, finite and infinite, temporal and eternal, and so on—but one in particular is relevant here. In confessing sin, the self, for the first time, becomes conscious of itself in all its inwardness. No longer is there any external power to tell the self its fate or to absolve it, for a while, of its guilt. The self is guilty, and it has no recourse but repentance, a death of the self in which the only remaining anxiety is over the possibility of deliverance from sin. Repentance is also the *Aufhebung* of the previous two phases in that it restores confession of sin as an unwarranted actuality at the same time that it acknowledges its own impotence to cancel sin. Repentance alone, no matter how profound, can never bring freedom (CA, 116).

In this final movement, anxiety in-and-for-itself, the first moment is anxiety about evil, in which anxiety is revealed as a "moment of death," for in it inwardness appears as total self-negation. The next moment introduces the demonic, which might seem startling after the discussion of repentance, but which in fact is dialectically coherent: the demonic negates the self-negation of repentance in a last effort at self-assertion. Rather than protest against the evil of sin, the demonic self protests against the good that has revealed sin to be sin: "The bondage of sin is an unfree relation to the evil, but the demonic is an unfree relation to the good" (CA, 119). When one sees that the only way to appropriate the good is to confess and repent of one's sin, a hostile reaction to the good can occur. Then "freedom is lost" (CA, 123), for the demonic individual denies the sinfulness of sin, rejects the rejection of sin, and negates the self-negation of repentance.

It is impossible to do justice here to Haufniensis's lengthy discussion of the demonic (CA, 118-54). Despite the obvious irony in his remark that "For me the principle thing is to have my schema in order" (CA, 137),[23] it is precisely the structure, as a dialectical

---

[23]The object of this barb is presumably not only Hegel but Kant, who defines schema as a "mediating representation" between logical categories and the intuitions of experience (*Critique of Pure Reason*, trans. Norman Kemp Smith [New York: St. Martin's Press, 1965] 181 [B 177/A 138]).

development of the experience of anxiety, that I shall analyze. There is less textual basis here than in previous sections of *The Concept of Anxiety* for a systematic analysis of phases. Nevertheless, it is possible to discern a dialectical development within the demonic.

In the first phase the demonic is treated abstractly, as a theoretical concept. Haufniensis discusses the three methods by which the demonic can be approached: aesthetic-metaphysical, ethical, and medical-therapeutic (CA, 119-23). The first sympathizes with the demonic that is determined by fate, the second condemns it, and the third treats it as a physical problem (in our terms, a matter of body chemistry). A number of characteristics of the demonic follow, each of which is discussed in some detail. The first is "withdrawnness," which "closes itself up within itself."[24] The withdrawn personality has not returned to external determinations; rather, inwardness here is given the intense perversity of one who rejects God, for "one cannot be withdrawn in God or in the good."[25] The other two characteristics of the demonic—the "sudden" and "the contentless, the boring" (CA, 129-33)—are described as new expressions for withdrawnness. Thus, there are three methods and three characteristics within the definition of the demonic, but no dialectical progression in either triad. To find such a progression, it is necessary to examine the ways in which demonic loss of freedom can be expressed.

The first way is "somatically-psychically," by which Haufniensis means what are now called psychosomatic conditions. He gives a number of examples, among them hysteria and hypochondria, and mentions very briefly that demoniacs often form extremely dependent relationships with one another, such that "no friendship has an inwardness that can be compared with it" (CA, 137).

---

[24]CA, 123-24; SV, 6:206-207. Kierkegaard's much-used word *Indesluttethed* means "reserve" or "reticence" in ordinary Danish, and literally implies "shut-upness." It has been translated "morbid reserve" (Lowrie), "inclosing reserve" (Thomte and Hong), and "isolation" (Thompson). I prefer to use "withdrawnness," in part because it, like the Danish, is an ordinary word with a technical (psychological) application, not a technical phrase unrelated to ordinary speech.

[25]CA, 133-34; SV, 6:216.

Even more illuminating is his description of how the psychosomatic demoniac deviates from a healthy relation to the good: "The body is the organ of the psyche and in turn the organ of the spirit. As soon as the serving relation comes to an end, as soon as the body revolts, and as soon as freedom conspires with the body against itself, unfreedom is present as the demonic" (CA, 136). The striking phrase here is "freedom conspires with the body against itself." This can be rendered more intelligible by recalling the place of the demonic within the dialectic of anxiety. The self has already achieved the inwardness of repentance, understood as the freedom that comes from encountering in God the good by which the self realizes its own sinfulness. That experience was accomplished in the first moment within anxiety in-and-for-itself. Then comes the demonic, which is the negation of that encounter, not by a return to externality but by a perversion of inwardness, namely, a withdrawnness of the self from God or the good. Rather than rest in the painful freedom of repentance, the self strives for independence from God. Thus, the demonic self is inwardly at war with itself, pitting its own autonomy against the freedom of the good, and it is this battle that allows freedom to conspire with the body against itself. The result is that the self's freedom appears to be lost psychosomatically, in some sort of debilitating nervous disorder. This inward self-alienation is the demonic for-itself, in contrast to the abstract definition of the demonic in-itself.

The other way in which the demoniac loses freedom is "pneumatically," in which freedom conspires not with the body but with the mind. The serving relation here is destroyed by the lack of consistency between the beliefs that the self espouses and the behavior that reflects the self's genuine inwardness: "truth is for the particular individual only as he himself produces it in action" (CA, 138). In a passage as typical of Haufniensis's convoluted style as it is expressive of his anti-Hegelian distinction between concrete existence and the philosophical "pure self-consciousness," he writes,

> The most concrete content that consciousness can have is consciousness of itself, of the individual himself—not the pure self-consciousness, but the self-consciousness that is so concrete that no author, not even the one with the greatest power of description, has ever been able to describe a single such self-conscious-

ness, although every single human being is such a one. This self-consciousness is not contemplation, for he who believes this has not understood himself, because he sees that meanwhile he himself is in the process of becoming and consequently cannot be something completed for contemplation. This self-consciousness, therefore, is action, and this action is in turn inwardness, and whenever inwardness does not correspond to this consciousness, there is a form of the demonic as soon as the absence of inwardness expresses itself as anxiety about its acquisition (CA, 143).

With many examples, Haufniensis illuminates what he means by this demonic anxiety over inwardness. In each of them, the basic conflict within the self is between passivity and activity. Thus, when the demonic self-inconsistency is one of unbelief *versus* superstition, these elements can be understood in their dialectical relation as equally lacking in inwardness: "unbelief is passive through an activity, and superstition is active through a passivity. . . . Superstition is unbelieving about itself. Unbelief is superstitious about itself" (CA, 144). In all of these formulations, self-reflection is shown to contradict the action of inwardness. The person who espouses unbelief on the grounds of a humanistic philosophy of action is rendered passive by virtue of a superstitious belief in the autonomy and capacity of the self. Conversely, the superstitious self appears to be passive, but its refusal to see its own active role as interpreter of omens (like the pagan receiving the oracle) constitutes a profound form of unbelief. Haufniensis mentions two other internal struggles between belief and action: "hypocrisy is offense at oneself, while offense is hypocrisy to oneself," and "pride is a profound cowardice. . . . [cowardice] is a profound pride" (CA, 145).

Haufniensis's concluding remarks on the demonic illuminate its dialectical role within anxiety in-and-for-itself. In his view, the demonic rejection of the good is a loss of inwardness, since inwardness is "eternity or the determination of the eternal in a man."[26] The pneumatic demoniac is one who intellectually con-

---

[26]CA, 151; SV, 6:231. To declare that one who refuses to repent is *ipso facto* demonic presupposes that the self is both created by God (and therefore essentially dependent) and also fundamentally free (and therefore responsible for choosing itself). As Louis Dupré remarks, "Kierkegaard is the first philosopher to place man's relation to God in the very heart of the self" (*A Dubious Heritage: Studies in the Philosophy of Religion after Kant* [New York: Paulist Press, 1977] 49).

ceives of countless evasions of the eternal, whereas the psychosomatic demoniac rejects the eternal by allowing the body to revolt
against the soul and spirit, thereby making inward consciousness
of the eternal impossible. Thus, the demonic constitutes a negation of the inwardness of repentance, which means that it is self-
assertion over against the inwardness of the eternal, the good. In
this sense, Haufniensis is consistent in calling the demonic a loss
of inwardness. But it is not a return to the externality of anxiety for-
itself, which is a total lack of consciousness of sin. As a rebellion
against God and a repudiation of the fact of sin, the demonic is an
attempt to assert the self's independence of the good, not by virtue
of an external relation to it but in unremitting opposition to it.
Without the consciousness of the eternal and of sin, there could be
no demonic. That is why I prefer to call it a perversion of inwardness rather than an absence of inwardness. The demonic is a futile
attempt to sustain inwardness and freedom without the good,
which is their origin and only sustaining power. As such, it is a false
inwardness and a form of unfreedom.

It is more difficult to trace the vague dialectical development of
phases within the demonic. Such as it is, that structure substanti-
ates the claim that the demonic is not so much an absence of inwardness as its perversion. The demonic in-itself is first defined as
withdrawnness, in which the self acknowledges no relational determinations. It closes in upon itself in the illusion of self-suffi-
ciency. In the demonic for-itself, that abstract unity of
withdrawnness is sundered, for the self finds itself at war with its
own body. This battle may be utterly internal, but it is nevertheless
violently divisive for the self. For the psychosomatic, the body becomes the external expression of an inner illness. The pneumatic
demonic reconciles this division, in the sense that the expression
of inward self-contradiction can no longer be identified with the
"external" body; now it is the self's action, a manifestation of inwardness no less than of consciousness that reveals that the self is
demonically at war with itself.

The demonic, as anxiety about the good, stands in opposition
to anxiety about evil, which resulted in repentance. This opposition is overcome by anxiety as saving through faith, which is the
subject of chapter 5. The primary argument in that short chapter is

that through faith it can be seen that anxiety is educative, for it is anxiety over possibility that leads the self along this difficult path to faith, a path on which every finite definition of the self is exposed as illusion until at last the self accepts itself as determined by the eternal (CA, 155-56).

There is an interesting and significant aspect of Haufniensis's analysis of faith, one that illustrates its dialectical development with striking clarity: the phases of faith recapitulate the moments of anxiety over the possibility of sin (chapter 3). Haufniensis first discusses the case of the person who has never been conscious of anxiety, that is, spiritlessness (CA, 157). If such a one is indeed "educated by possibility" (CA, 158), then the possibility of faith will also appear: "Then the assaults of anxiety, even though they be terrifying, will not be such that he flees from them. For him, anxiety becomes a serving spirit that against its will leads him where he wishes to go" (CA, 159). This situation is the positing of anxiety as educative, in systematic terms, of faith in-itself. It is followed by a second phase, faith for-itself, in which anxiety discovers fate: "but just when the individual wants to put his trust in fate, anxiety turns around and takes fate away, because fate is like anxiety, and anxiety, like possibility, is a 'magic' picture" (CA, 159). Fate, of course, is the second moment within anxiety over the possibility of actual sin. Whereas the pagan remains shackled by fate, the Christian learns that anxiety leads beyond it too. "With the help of faith, anxiety brings up the individuality to rest in providence" (CA, 161). Finally, anxiety discovers the guilt that lies beyond fate. Here the lesson of faith is that "he who in relation to guilt is educated by anxiety will rest only in the Atonement" (CA, 162).

The dialectic here is as follows: faith in-itself posits anxiety as saving through faith; faith for-itself is the last flicker of negation and otherness, in which salvation is identified with Providence in a relatively external manner; and faith in-and-for-itself is the at-one-ment of the self with the eternal, in which "the eternal in man" is fully realized.

The concept of the eternal in man thus points toward the internalization of consciousness of the divine eternal other. God is known only inwardly, although he remains other to human inwardness. This conclusion, together with the crucial role played by sin-consciousness, confirms also that *The Concept of Anxiety* deals primarily with the religious stage. Finally, the systematic dialectical structure of Haufniensis's argument should by now be clear. All that remains is to describe briefly how that structure is manifest both within the final movement (anxiety over the actuality of sin) and among the three movements of the text as a whole. Following that description, a summary chart will outline the entire structure, characterizing each movement, moment, and phase and correlating each (in brackets) with the chapters and sections of *The Concept of Anxiety*.

Faith is the third moment of the third movement, which is anxiety in-and-for-itself. The way in which this movement unfolds can be described as follows: in anxiety about evil, inwardness is posited as a "moment of death," a confession of sin and an impotent repentance that constitute the self's negation of itself before the goodness of the eternal. In a form of self-assertion, the demonic opposes this self-negation by its denial of the hegemony of the eternal. The reconciliation of these two moments in faith can be characterized as a self-affirmation of the self as dependent upon God. With the first moment, faith acknowledges the self's dependence upon God; with the second, it affirms the self; the two moments are *aufgehoben* in such a way as to negate the abject self-negation of the first moment and the proud self-assertion of the second (the demonic).

Finally, the structure of *The Concept of Anxiety* as a whole demonstrates that it does, indeed, reflect a systematic development of inwardness. In anxiety in-itself, inwardness is still in an embryonic form, for the self's anxiety is projected onto external others—whether indeterminate, the created world, or the erotic other. Consciousness of inwardness first appears as the consciousness of the self over against or in relation to the eternal as externally manifest. This is anxiety for-itself, in which the eternal is never fully internalized; it is ignored (Christendom), externally determined (paganism), or externally expressed (Judaism). In anxiety in-and-for-itself, the eternal as the determination of inwardness is revealed in the dialectic of self-negation (confession and repentance of sin), self-assertion (the demonic), and self-affirmation in dependence upon God (faith). Thus, the three movements of the dialectic of anxiety can be analyzed as follows: an initial, abstract unity in which the self has not yet consciously distinguished itself from its external world; a negative dialectic of opposition between the self as inner and an external power that determines it; and a final reconciliation in which the determining power is inwardly revealed and appropriated and the self finds in faith the culmination and fulfillment of its dialectical education by anxiety.

The Dialectic of Inwardness in The Concept of Anxiety

A. Anxiety posited as origin and result of sin
   1. Dreaming anxiety: self seeks itself in indeterminate other [1]
   2. Objective anxiety: self projects anxiety onto nonhuman other (creation) [2.1]
   3. Subjective anxiety: self finds itself in relation to human other [2.2]
      a. Modesty: alien erotic (self not related to its other)
      b. Propagation: comic erotic (self related to its other)
      c. Christianity: suspended erotic (self identical with its other)

ANXIETY IN-ITSELF:
SELF'S INNER ANXIETY PROJECTED
ONTO EXTERNAL OTHER

B. Anxiety over the possibility of actual sin [3]
   1. Spiritlessness in Christendom: anxiety waiting (consciousness repressed) [3.1]
   2. Dialectic of fate in paganism: inner anxiety about external oracle [3.2]
   3. Dialectic of guilt in Judaism: inner anxiety expressed in external sacrifice [3.3]

ANXIETY FOR-ITSELF:
DIALECTIC IN WHICH SELF IS DETERMINED
BY EXTERNAL RELATION TO THE ETERNAL

C. Anxiety over the actuality of sin
   1. Anxiety about evil: inwardness as self-negation [4.1]
      a. Sin posited as unwarranted actuality (sophistical claim of freedom)
      b. Compromise with sin (impotence to achieve freedom from sin)

    c. Repentance of sin (impotent sorrow in hope of freedom)
2. Anxiety about good: demonic self-assertion [4.2]
    a. Withdrawnness into self
    b. Psychosomatic externalization of self
    c. Spiritual self-contradiction within self
3. Anxiety as saving by means of faith: self-affirmation in depen-
    dence on God [5]
    a. Spirit as the eternal within the self (*vs.* spiritlessness)
    b. Providence as the eternal over the self (*vs.* fate)
    c. Atonement reconciles the eternal with the self (*vs.* guilt)

ANXIETY IN-AND-FOR-ITSELF:
SELF CONSTITUTED IN INWARDNESS

II

Kierkegaard's "Anxiety" and the Augustinian Doctrine of Original Sin

by Lee Barrett

I f one does not take the importance of the "mood" of the discrete enterprises of dogmatics and psychology into account, Kierkegaard's treatment of original sin and such related concerns as freedom, responsibility, and grace is baffling. Several generations of scholars have puzzled over certain apparent incongruities in his work. On the one hand, Kierkegaard frequently associates all sin, including "original," with the guilt that can only arise from the free act, or "leap," of an individual. In fact, the importance of the "moment" of the individual's responsible decision is clearly one of the dominant themes of his entire authorship. Ostensibly, it seems that to attribute a religiously significant "act" to someone is to identify him as the author of what is brought about and to ascribe responsibility for it to him. To be responsible seems to entail that the act be voluntary, that is, that the individual was (or should have been) aware of the circumstances of the act and of possible alternative courses of action, and that the act was performed intentionally. No internal or external antecedent condition can be a reason for withholding praise or blame from the individual.

But, on the other hand, Kierkegaard is quite capable of describing sin as a "state" in which an individual is born seemingly prior to any obvious personal decision. Moreover, this "sin" seems to be universal and to possess a suprapersonal quality. At least three different issues are involved here. If sin is a guilty "leap," that is, a free act, it seems that it can only be a characteristic of individual acts, and not an enduring characteristic of the agent. "State" seems to suggest a condition that endures through its own momentum rather than through the efforts of the individual. The past history of the state somehow accounts for its continuation in the present, without reference to the present intentional activity of the agent. For example, an individual's current state of depression may be explained by the fact that he has been depressed for three weeks. This does not mean that he has decided each morning to be depressed, or that something new has caused the depression each morning. Rather, depression is the sort of thing that can perpetuate itself without the voluntary activity of the agent. Thus, the continuation of a state seems to fall outside the realm of the agent's responsibility. This sort of "state" might qualify as an antecedent condition that would prevent the ascription of responsibility for sin to the individual. Second, at most it seems that an individual could be held responsible for the inception of a state. Possibly the individual could do something to produce such states as depression or drunkenness. If this is the case, responsibility for a "state" of sin could not be attributed to any individual until that individual has reached a sufficient level of cognitive and volitional maturity to make responsible decisions. Consequently, applying "sinner" to infants and children would be absolutely inappropriate. Third, if all sinful guilt is personal, all talk of "corporate sin" would be unintelligible.

This apparent tension between "sin" as an individual decision and sin as a suprapersonal state has led some scholars to propose that Kierkegaard entertained two contradictory notions of sin.

Torsten Bohlin, for example, suggested that in *The Sickness unto Death* and *The Concept of Anxiety* Kierkegaard operates with a definition of sin as a guilty decision, while in *Philosophical Fragments* and *Concluding Unscientific Postscript* he advances a more "dogmatic" view of sin as a corruption of human nature.[1] Similarly, G. E. and G. B. Arbaugh detect "an apparently contradictory duality" in Kierkegaard's claims that guilt must arise from free choice and that, nevertheless, original sin involves "inherited" guilt.[2] Louis Dupré also suggests that Kierkegaard is "laboring with two concepts which he is unable to harmonize completely," "the orthodox protestant doctrine," in which original sin does involve guilt, and a Hegelian view of "spirit," in which original sin is a stage of consciousness.[3]

Alternatively, some scholars have seized upon either the "leap" theme or the "state" theme and used the one to reinterpret (or explain away) the other. One group focuses upon the "state" motif in Kierkegaard's appropriation of the dogmatic description of the condition of the race and identifies it with such psychological phenomena as anxiety or guilt-consciousness. Thus, Kresten Nordentoft stresses the dogmatic suprapersonal conception of guilt in the pages of Kierkegaard and concludes that original sin is not due to the free, responsible action of individuals, but is an ontological condition that individuals only "discover." The "leap" mentioned in *The Concept of Anxiety* is not really a leap into sin but is rather a leap into the sin-consciousness discussed in *The Sickness unto Death*.[4] James Loder and J. P. Cole exhibit similar beliefs.[5] In their approach, original sin is indeed "sin," but it loses the character of an

---

[1]Torsten Bohlen, *Kierkegaard's dogmatiska åskådning i dess historiska sammanhang* (Stockholm: Diakonistyrelses Förlag, 1925).

[2]G. E. and G. B. Arbaugh, *Kierkegaard's Authorship* (Rock Island IL: Augustana College Library, 1967) 168-69.

[3]Louis Dupré, *Kierkegaard as Theologian* (New York: Sheed and Ward, 1963) 61.

[4] Kresten Nordentoft, *Kierkegaard's Psychology* (Pittsburgh: Duquesne University Press, 1978) 168-74.

[5]J. Preston Cole, *The Problematic Self in Kierkegaard and Freud* (New Haven: Yale University Press, 1971); James Loder, *Religious Pathology and Christian Faith* (Philadelphia: Westminster Press, 1966).

act for which the individual is responsible. In fact, the doctrine of original sin in Kierkegaard is usually found to be compatible with causal accounts of human action.

Other commentators have focused on the "sin as a decisive act" aspect of Kierkegaard's thought and concluded that original sin as a state really fails to satisfy the criteria for true guilt and sin. Mark Taylor, for example, emphasizes Kierkegaard's apparent polemic against traditional deterministic views of sin as an inherited state and concludes that Kierkegaard wanted to identify original sin with the nonmoral psychological state of dread prior to the individual's properly sinful acts.[6] S. U. Zuidema puts this thesis most starkly, proposing that "he [Kierkegaard] modifies the doctrine of original sin so that it is compatible with his extreme individualism. His adherence to this doctrine is purely verbal: in reality it is denied."[7] Common to this approach is the reasoning that genuine sin, according to Kierkegaard, must be the free act of an individual. An enduring state cannot be rooted in a deliberate individual decision; consequently, original sin can only be a nonmoral psychological phenomenon involving no guilt.

Evidently there is a great deal of disagreement about the significance of Kierkegaard's use of the Augustinian-Lutheran doctrine of original sin. One party claims that he entertained contradicting opinions, another party proposes that he believed that original sin is indeed sin because he did not really insist upon individual responsibility when writing as a Christian, and a final party suggests that he rejected the notion that original sin is true sin because he did insist upon individual responsibility. The last two groups are agreed that if "original sin" is a "state," it cannot involve individual responsibility; they only disagree as to whether sin does require that kind of responsibility.

I shall argue that it is indeed true that both the "leap" and the "state" motifs are present in Kierkegaard's writings about original sin. On the one hand, Kierkegaard is quite capable of remarking,

---

[6]Mark Taylor, *Kierkegaard's Pseudonymous Authorship* (Princeton: Princeton University Press, 1975) 268-73.

[7]S. U. Zuidema, *Kierkegaard* (Grand Rapids: Baker Book House, 1960) 21.

"Original sin is guilt—that is the real paradox" (JP, 2:1530). On the other hand, the "thin" pseudonym Vigilius can say, "It is nevertheless true that every individual becomes guilty only through himself" (CA, 53). I shall argue that proper attention to the purposes and "moods" of these remarks will help resolve this apparent contradiction. Kierkegaard did not regard the concepts "state" and "responsible act" as incompatible. He believed that the problem of integrating "act" and "state" language with regard to sin actually had two distinguishable aspects, one pertaining to the dogmatic description of the individual's identity, and one pertaining to the psychological exploration of the passional sources of sinfulness. Part of his program involved carefully distinguishing the proper moods and tasks of psychology and dogmatics (as well as immanent ethics). The problem of relating "state" language and "act" language must be considered in each domain separately before the two domains can be integrated. Much confusion has resulted from applying the "state" talk appropriate to dogmatics to the "state" talk of psychology, and vice versa.

The Concept of Anxiety explores the "state" and "leap" aspects of original sin by establishing boundaries between psychology and dogmatics. Significantly, the motto that prefaces the work laments, "The age of making distinctions is past. It has been vanquished by the system" (CA, 3). A paean to Socrates, the maker of distinctions, recalls this theme at the book's conclusion. The contrast between obfuscating systems and clarifying distinctions pervades the introduction and first chapter. The first paragraph of the introduction warns of the "deliberation" that "forgets where it properly belongs" (CA, 9), and the last paragraph of the first chapter notes that the book will not please "the admired men of science" whose "concern in their search after the system is known to the whole congregation" (CA, 59). Throughout these sections Vigilius warns of the pernicious effects of confusing such concepts of logic as "immediacy" and "the negative" with such concepts of dogmatics as "faith" and "evil." The point of these remarks is unmistakable: each domain of discourse must keep to its proper boundaries. As Niels Thulstrup has shown, the immediate occasion for Kierkegaard's concern was Hegel's, Marheineke's, and Martensen's attempts to arrange all the academic disciplines, including psychology, dogmatics, and ethics, according to the dictates of an ontological logic.[8] But, according to Vigilius, no "system" can homogenize all these domains of discourse without violating the meaning of the original concepts.

The meaning of a concept is embedded in its relationships with other concepts from the same domain. For example, the concept "knight" has a certain use in chess. In order to grasp this, one must see how "knight" is part of a particular conceptual network, how knights behave in relation to "pawn," "rook," and many other concepts. Concepts from a linguistic domain other than chess will not clarify the meaning of "knight." For example, the concept "molecular structure" from the linguistic domain of chemistry cannot elucidate "knight." The meaning of "knight" does not depend on an analysis of its chemical composition. Similarly, the meaning of "sin" can only be given in relation to such concepts as "atonement," "incarnation," and "creation," all from the same linguistic domain. As Kierkegaard suggests in *Training in Christianity* and *Concluding Unscientific Postscript*, "sin" is not the name of any particular unethical deed or set of deeds, but refers to the way in which all of an individual's activities and passivities predispose him to be offended at the God incarnate in Jesus. Understanding such a concept as "sin" cannot be achieved by taking the concept out of its natural domain and locating it in a putative trans-domain "system."

Each domain has its proper "mood," and the mood of its discourse is intrinsic to the meaning of its constitutive concepts. Here "mood" suggests a passional quality that accompanies the linguistic and nonlinguistic activities typical of that domain of discourse. Vigilius writes, "That science, just as much as poetry and art, presupposes a mood in the creator as well as in the observer, and that an error in the modulation is just as disturbing as an error in the development of thought, have been entirely forgotten in our time" (CA, 14). Vigilius's statement emphasizes that the meaning of a concept is dependent upon the passional qualities of the situation in which it is typically used. For example, "mother" is not

---

[8]Niels Thulstrup, *Kierkegaard's Relation to Hegel* (Princeton: Princeton University Press, 1980) 351-55.

a passion-neutral name used to identify some individual. To understand the concept "mother" is to recognize its typical use in such emotion-laden contexts as expressing filial affection or parental obligation. If a person did not seem to realize that people normally express some sort of concern upon learning that their mother is ill, his understanding of the concept "mother" could be doubted. Similarly, to apply the concept "shepherd" to God is not to report a passion-neutral fact like "Mr. Jones is a shepherd," but is to express an attitude of trust in God. It is not the case that the concepts in these instances have a meaning first cognitively grasped and only subsequently translated into pathos. Rather, understanding the concept requires using it with the proper kind of pathos. In using such concepts in the appropriate situations, the speaker may be expressing something, trying to evoke some emotional response from the hearer, and so forth. These activities must occur in the appropriate situation. "God help us," for example, must be said when the circumstances are dire. Kierkegaard uses "mood" to call attention to these vital passional characteristics intrinsic to the meaning of a concept. Because each domain of discourse requires its proper mood, confusion inevitably results whenever a concept is taken from one domain and transferred to another domain with its differing mood, or to some putative metadomain (system) that really has no particular mood at all. This importance of "mood," which Vigilius stresses throughout the text, has profound consequences for the treatment of original sin.

The primary project of the introduction and first chapter of *The Concept of Anxiety* is to identify the proper domain of discourse and mood for "original sin" and to map its possible relations to relevant concepts from other domains. In order to accomplish this, Vigilius delimits the respective territories of psychology, ethics, and dogmatics. The purpose of the book is "the sense in which the subject of our deliberations is a task of psychological interest and the sense in which, after having been the task and interest of psychology, it points directly to dogmatics" (CA, 9).

Although the concept "ethical guilt" has some affinities with "sin," "original sin" is not a concept indigenous to ethics. Ethics articulates an ideal way of life and exhorts individuals to actualize this ideal. The imperative mood assumes that the individual has the capacity to actualize the idea and regards failures to do so as accidental episodes that must be avoided in the future. Ethics, as an "ideal science," regards "guilt" as a quality of particular acts that says nothing about the fundamental moral capabilities of the agent. In fact, the actual moral condition of the agent is irrelevant to the mood of ethical ideality (CA, 16).

Nor is psychology the proper home of "original sin." Vigilius insists, "Sin, however, is no subject for psychological concern, and only by submitting to the service of a misplaced brilliance could it be dealt with psychologically" (CA, 14). Psychology, like ethics, lacks the requisite mood. In a mood of observation and curiosity, psychology examines "states" of human subjectivity. Vigilius notes, "The subject of which psychology treats must be something in repose that remains in restless repose" (CA, 21). Psychology can explore the inner dynamics of any subjective condition and even examine the unresolved tensions that might motivate a movement to another emotional state. However, a mood of observation cannot "understand" the actual movement, for movement requires passionate concern rather than observation. Therefore, if sin is a "movement," psychology can never hope to explain it. Vigilius warns, "If sin is dealt with in psychology, the mood becomes that of persistent observation, like the fearlessness of a secret agent, but not that of a victorious flight of earnestness out of sin" (CA, 15).

Rather, "original sin" is a concept appropriate to dogmatics. In fact, it is one of the foundational concepts of the Christian life. As such, it is logically primitive and cannot be reduced without remainder to any concept drawn from a different domain of discourse. Vigilius writes, "Therefore dogmatics must not explain hereditary sin but rather explain it by presupposing it, like that vortex about which Greek speculation concerning nature had so much to say" (CA, 20). Vigilius's theme of original sin as the "presupposition" of dogmatics is repeated throughout Kierkegaard's writings. In his journals, he remarks, "That I exist (er til) was the eternal presupposition of the ancient world: that I am a sinner is the new spontaneity of the Christian consciousness: the one can be demonstrated no more than the other" (JP, 1:1032). Similarly, Climacus in *Philosophical Fragments* and *Concluding Unscientific Postscript* argues that the "dialectical" and "revealed" concepts of

Christianity, including "sin," are not reducible to the immanental concepts of general human pathos (Religion A).

Kierkegaard's reflections about "presuppositional" concepts resemble the remarks of certain analytic philosophers about the "epistemic autonomy" of the concepts of distinctive language-games. As William Alston proposes, the basic concepts of any truly distinctive language-game form a "closed circle," making the definition of these concepts in terms of concepts drawn from outside the game impossible.[9] For example, "physical object" can never be exhaustively defined in terms of the sense-data game, and "purpose" can never be exhaustively defined in terms of the causal-necessity game. The employment of the concept "ball" is not reducible to talk about neurological events. In the same way, language about "original sin" is not reducible to talk about ethical guilt or psychological states. Such foundational concepts as "duty" of the ethical domain and "object" of the physical domain are not derived from the propositions of other domains. Rather, they regulate new and different ways of thinking, feeling, and behaving. In regard to their own domains, they are primitive in the way that "I" is primitive for general discourse. In Kierkegaard's more picturesque terminology, they are "Archimedian points."

In general, this "epistemic autonomy" of doctrine led Kierkegaard to accept the logically primitive concepts of the Augustinian-Lutheran language-game. He writes in his journals, "On the whole, the doctrine as it is presented is quite correct. I have no quarrel with this. My contention is that something should be made of it" (JP, 6:7602). Unsurprisingly, Vigilius applauds the tradition's teachings about original sin, particularly for expressing the enormity of sin. He admires the Smalkald Articles' "pious feeling that gives vent to its indignation over hereditary sin," and notes that it is correct in insisting that sin cannot be comprehended by human understanding (CA, 26). The Formula of Concord likewise possesses "the eloquence of the contrite soul" in denouncing original sin as "guilt, sin, vice, and transgression" (CA, 27). Similarly, in his journals

---

[9]William Alston, "The Christian Language Game," in *The Autonomy of Religious Belief*, ed. Frederick Crossan (Notre Dame: University of Notre Dame Press, 1981) 133-38.

Kierkegaard praises Augustine for recognizing that concupiscence and ignorance are not tragic debilities but are themselves sin, and, as such, culpable (JP, 4:4047). These comments suggest that Kierkegaard had no fundamental objections to what he perceived to be the doctrine of original sin in the Augustinian-Lutheran tradition. He had no interest in being a doctrinal revisionist; he only wanted to insure that the doctrine would be appropriated in the proper mood of passionate self-concern that gives it meaning.

Without the mood of "earnestness," the doctrine of original sin cannot be understood. Vigilius insists that understanding "sin" requires repenting of it and struggling against it. The activities of exhortation, self-scrutiny, and contrition are ingredient to the meaning of the concept. Sin's proper context is the sermon "in which the single individual speaks as a single individual to the single individual" (CA, 16). The proper mood resides in this situation of being personally accused and convicted. If the mood proper to the concept is ever forgotten, "the concept is altered, and thereby the mood that properly corresponds to the concept is also disturbed, and instead of the endurance of the true mood there is the fleeting phantom of false moods" (CA, 14). The proper mood is not automatically generated by a "neutral" understanding of the concept. "Sin" is not a passion-neutral description of any set of behaviors or emotions. Rather, developing the appropriate mood is intrinsic to grasping the meaning of "sin."

Essential to the proper mood of "original sin" is the passionate assumption of responsibility for one's deeds. Here Vigilius's emphasis of the "leap" character of sin is crucial. Any attempt to "explain" sin by looking for necessitating antecedent conditions would engender a mood inimical to the true concept. Causal explanations presuppose a mood of curious detachment that shifts responsibility away from the individual. Vigilius wants to insure that psychology will recognize its boundary and not entangle dogmatics in deterministic explanations. He cautions, "Psychology can bring its concern to the point where it seems as if sin is there, but the next thing, that sin is there, is qualitatively different from the first" (CA, 22). The logic of action cannot be incorporated into any explanatory scheme without destroying the mood that gives it meaning.

When the proper mood of self-concern and responsibility is present, the traditional doctrine of original sin can acquire meaning as the individual learns to employ it in seeing himself and others in new ways. The meaning of the doctrine depends upon its correct application in the life of the individual. The doctrine should enable the individual to answer the question "Why do I do what I do?" The doctrine's answer, however, is not logically on a par with any psychological explanation. "Why" here does not seek an answer in terms of psychological motivations. The concept "because" has a different force in this context; it is not an alternative to the psychological "because." Vigilius remarks, "by means of hereditary sin it [dogmatics] explains the sin of the single individual" (CA, 20). Original sin "explains" the particular sins of particular individuals not by searching for predisposing antecedent conditions, but by placing these particular sins in a new conceptual framework.

The doctrine involves seeing "sins" as part of the typical, expected behavior of human agents. Kierkegaard observes in a journal entry, "On the whole, as I see it, 'original sin' is an expression of the fact that Christianity uses God's standard. God sees everything *in uno*" (JP, 4:4035). The individual learns to employ this standard and to regard sin from a unifying perspective. Primarily, the doctrine is a rule for regarding all of one's own actions. The doctrinal answer to the question "Why do I sin?" is that I sin because I am and always have been the sort of person who would sin. An individual misdeed should not be regarded as an exception to one's general goodness. This theme informs Vigilius's discussion of the relation of the "leap" and the "quality" in the "first sin" of Adam. The story of Adam, which is the story of us all, depicts the archetypal relation of the sinful act to the sinful "quality" of the agent. Since "the first sin constitutes the nature of the quality" (CA, 30), it is not just one particular act in a series of equally significant acts. Rather, this act establishes a new "quality" in the agent. One has not merely done a bad deed; one has become a bad person.

Kierkegaard is suggesting that within the Christian system of discourse, certain acts determine an individual's very identity. Analogously, in secular talk about persons, one might identify Mr. X by saying, "He is a murderer." This description does not mean that Mr. X is committing a murder at this very moment, much less that he habitually murders at every moment. Nevertheless, one still does not hesitate to refer today to Mr. X as a murderer although it was three weeks ago that he performed the deed. The significance of such an act as murder in our civil life gives it an agent-identification role. According to Kierkegaard, in Christian discourse sin is infinitely significant and identifies the individual as a unified agent.

It is not the case that only the first sinful deed establishes the quality, and that subsequent sins should be understood "quantitatively," as repetitions of the same thing. Adam's "first sin" depicts the relation of "leap" and "quality" in every sinful act in the life of an individual, not merely in an isolable initial episode. Every act must be viewed as identifying the agent as "sinner." Every deed, construed according to the story of Adam as a fall from innocence, should be regarded with infinite seriousness.

On the other hand, Vigilius also asserts that the leap "is presupposed by the quality" (CA, 32). The act (leap) of sin not only establishes a new quality, but also manifests what the individual has been all along. The act is taken to be revelatory of the individual's identity; the individual is that kind of person. For example, to see an individual as being essentially a "murderer" would involve regarding that person's past uncontrollable bursts of anger, flagrant disregard of others' welfare, and so forth, as culminating in that deed. Of course, not all acts are revelatory of an individual's character; some are atypical and require special explanations. According to Kierkegaard, the doctrine of original sin should be used to focus upon sinful episodes as revealing the implicit dynamics of our lives as a whole, extending back to our preconscious choices.

In general, Vigilius is proposing two things about the relation of identity and acts. Certain acts establish one's identity, and one's identity is expressed in certain acts. The doctrine of original sin requires that one see individual sins as expressions of one's true character, as well as regard one's sinful character as the result of one's own acts. In the first sin of Adam, the quality presupposes the leap, and the leap presupposes the quality. Thus, the doctrine of original sin serves to unify the deeds of the agent, to see them "in uno." This unity of the agent as sinner is not given through an inductive empirical survey of the agent's deeds; rather, it is one of the foundational concepts of the Christian faith.

Moreover, the doctrine not only unifies the agent's deeds, but also unites individuals in the "race." Individuals who seem lost in sin should be taken as revealing the awful truth about our own selves. Thus, the proper use of the doctrine does indeed have a "corporate" aspect. As Louis Dupré has noted, Kierkegaard, the seemingly rigorous individualist, could talk about the race as a unit.[10] According to Vigilius, just as Adam was an individual and yet also the entire human race, so also each individual is "both himself and the race" (CA, 29). Vigilius frequently quotes the Latin proverb "*unum noris omnes*" (CA, 79). In fact, Climacus proposes that Christianity paradoxically makes the "race" higher than the individual (CUP, 492). This solidarity of the race in sin is one of the ground rules of the faith and is not based upon empirical observation. Vigilius observes, "It is obvious that our subject is not one that may occupy physicians, such as whether one is born deformed, etc., nor is the subject that of arriving at results by tabulated surveys" (CA, 62).

The corporate use of the doctrine should only serve to heighten the mood of the individual's responsibility for his own guilt. Contemplating the sins of the race should always be used to redirect the individual's attention to the gravity of his own state. The race reveals the depravity of the individual's own self. After affirming that the universality of sin must be believed, Kierkegaard adds, "Beyond that I have to concentrate my earnestness solely on this— that I am a sinner" (JP, 4:4038). The doctrine of corporate sinfulness only makes sense in the context of passionate concern for one's own self in the eyes of God. Without this concern, the doctrine will be misunderstood as a deterministic "system" and used as an excuse for the sins of the individual.

This analysis of the agent-identification and character-manifestation uses of the doctrine of original sin enables Kierkegaard to apply both "act" language and "state" language to it. The "leap" (act) quality of original sin is dependent upon the proper mood of

---

[10]Dupré, *Kierkegaard as Theologian*, 51-52, 59-61.

self-ascription of responsibility. Responsibility for sin is not based on any neutral demonstration that the individual is indeed the "cause" of sin. Rather, "responsibility" is intrinsic to the very meaning of the concept. Kierkegaard does not try to justify his regarding the individual as a sinner, but tries to engender the pathos necessary for understanding the concept. The "state" language appears in the pathos-laden uses to which the doctrine is put. Particular episodes are seen as establishing a continuous identity. The proper mood requires that the responsibility appropriate to an act be extended to the entirety of one's life.

Thus, Kierkegaard distinguishes the tasks of ethics, psychology, and dogmatics and proposes that dogmatics is an autonomous linguistic domain that has meaning when, in the proper mood, it is applied to an individual's life. The respective concerns of ethics, psychology, and dogmatics are all legitimate as long as each remains within its proper boundaries. Kierkegaard does not want to eliminate psychology in the interest of dogmatics, or to regard dogmatics as allegorized psychology. Each domain has its appropriate and distinctive task.

Although neither ethics, psychology, nor dogmatics can be reduced to one of the others, they do impinge upon one another in ways significant for the "leap" and "state" aspects of "original sin." Without confusing the tasks of these discrete enterprises, Kierkegaard explores the relationships between the central concepts "ethical guilt," "anxiety," and "sin." The respective linguistic domains are not hermetically sealed off from one another. In fact, the ability to use "original sin" requires a certain facility with ethics and psychology. Kierkegaard examines the interconnections of dogmatics and "immanent" ethics in *Concluding Unscientific Postscript* and those of dogmatics and psychology in *The Concept of Anxiety*. This essay will concentrate upon the latter issue.

Before determining the exact nature of Kierkegaard's use of psychology in dogmatics, one must further explore his knowledge of and attitude toward the technical theology of the Augustinian-Lutheran tradition. Throughout his journals, Kierkegaard demonstrates a deep concern for the differences between Augustinianism, Pelagianism, and semi-Pelagianism exhibited in the debates between the Scholastics and Reformers. His familiarity with these controversies was not gleaned through careful study of the original sources, but from various textbooks of dogmatics and lectures on the history of doctrine. From 1833 to 1834 Kierkegaard attended the lectures on historical theology by H. N. Clausen, a mildly rationalistic Danish theologian influenced by Kant and Schleiermacher. Kierkegaard used these notes extensively while writing *The Concept of Anxiety*. He frequently referred to Karl Hase's *Hutterus Redivivus* and C. G. Bretschneider's *Handbuch der Dogmatik der evangelisch-lutherischen Kirche*. He also owned and probably used August Hahn's *Lehrbuch des Christlichen Glaubens*.[11] Although these authors differed theologically (Bretschneider was a mild "rationalist" while Hahn was a "supernaturalist"), their works organized and presented the doctrinal issues along very similar lines. From these works and Kierkegaard's references to them, Kierkegaard's picture of the historical development of the doctrine of original sin can be reconstructed.

Clausen, Hase, Bretschneider, and Hahn all agreed that the basic tenet of Augustinianism was the human inability to "produce the religious life" or the "feeling" of the divine presence through the self's own efforts. The longing for the experience of the presence of God is frustrated by the inherent incapacity of the self to actualize its own divine telos. Divine aid is absolutely necessary to overcome this debility. The textbooks interpreted the Augustinian position as requiring the noncooperation of the human will in the reception of grace. They also stressed Augustine's conviction that this disability involves both guilt and punishment, which are inherited and corporate. In order to explain the presence of the disability in Adam's posterity, Augustine used a biological metaphor and spoke of genetic transmission. The guilt of subsequent individuals, however, was explained in terms of the race's participation in Adam's particular act. Much of the Augustinian tradition devoted enormous intellectual energy to the problem of determining how exactly future generations participated in

---

[11]K. G. Bretschneider, *Handbuch der Dogmatik der evangelisch-lutherischen Kirche* (Leipzig: Barth, 1838); August Hahn, *Lehrbuch des christlichen Glaubens* (Leipzig: F. C. W. Vogel, 1828); Karl Hase, *Hutterus redivivus* (Leipzig: Breitkopf U. Härtel, 1839); *Søren Kierkegaards Papirer*, ed. Niels Thulstrup (Copenhagen: Gyldendal, 1968) vol. 12.

Adam's act. Kierkegaard could make use of the first two themes, but not the third.

The literature also devoted a great deal of attention to semi-Pelagianism, seeing it as a precursor to the synergist controversy between Matthias Flacius and Victorin Strigel that had divided Lutheranism in the last half of the sixteenth century. The textbooks traced the history of this semi-Pelagianism from Cassian through the Scholastics and claimed to detect it in the Council of Trent. The common feature of all this semi-Pelagianism was the "synergistic" contention that the will can cooperate with grace in spite of the universal propensity to sin. The corruption of original sin is not total. The authors distinguished two different strategies by which the Scholastics salvaged some inherent rectitude of will. One, associated with Peter Lombard, identified the disability with concupiscence in the lower powers of the soul and maintained that these wayward desires do not become sin until they are adopted by the will. The other, associated with Anselm, regarded original sin as the loss of the *donum supernaturalis*, the supernatural knowledge of God and rectitude of will that Adam had enjoyed. This loss merely weakened human natural powers, leaving them still capable of performing morally good acts in the natural order. This Scholastic form of semi-Pelagianism was regarded as supporting the doctrine of congruous merit, the theory that certain acts, in spite of sin, could be performed, which God would reward with grace.

Lutheran orthodoxy emerges in the literature as a return to pure Augustinianism. The textbooks quote the confessional documents to show that original sin is completely debilitating. The Augsburg Confession, the Smalkaldic Articles, and the Formula of Concord agree that sin is much more than the disordering of the lower appetites or the loss of a special gift. Guilt and corruption infect all the components of a person, including the higher faculties of reason and will. Moreover, the rebellious instincts, even without the consent of the will, are not morally neutral but do involve guilt. The Apology of the Augsburg Confession and the Smalkaldic Articles stress the culpability of such affections as anger and doubt apart from any action of the will. The Lutheran tradition consistently rejected the distinction of natural and supernatural goods and regarded sinfulness as perverting all dimensions of human life.

The secondary literature did describe the many ways post-Reformation theology explained the nature of the individual's participation in original sin. Prominent among these theories was the view that Adam was a "real universal," the ideal form of humanity in which all subsequent individuals were contained. Another theory maintained that all individuals were "seminally" present in Adam's loins and therefore were responsible for his deed. Yet another, the federal theology, proposed that Adam, through a special covenant with God, was the legal representative of all people. The more moderate view of "mediate imputation" argued that God ascribes the guilt of Adam to all individuals only insofar as they declare their solidarity with Adam through their own personal sin. Another moderate view, employing the conceptual device of the "*scientia Dei media*" (God's knowledge of counterfactual hypotheticals), suggested that God foresaw that each individual, if placed in Adam's situation, would have sinned in the same manner as did Adam.

Mainstream Lutheranism, as these textbooks pointed out, tended to emphasize biological transmission and based the guilt of original sin upon the presence of inherited corruption in the soul, rather than upon participation in Adam's act. The Augsburg Confession, for example, claims that the corruption present in an individual at birth is sufficient for damnation, but makes no mention of participation in Adam's particular deed. Many of the major Lutheran theologians based this theory upon "traducianism," the view that the soul of the child is derived from that of the father (sometimes both parents). Chemnitz, Gerhard, and Quensted to varying degrees all supported the theory of the biological transmission of corruption and its concomitant guilt.

Kierkegaard accepted the traditional teachings about original sin as part of the foundational concepts of Christianity. He showed clear affinities with the confessional Lutheran tradition in its opposition to semi-Pelagianism, insisting that original sin involves a corruption of all capacities (not just the lower appetites), that it does entail guilt (and not just a nonculpable debility), and that it is universal. Haufniensis preferred the Lutheran formulations to the Scholastic attempts to regard original sin as the loss of original righteousness, punishment for sin, or nonsinful concupiscence.

However, Kierkegaard did fear that the tradition had confused the agent-description force of the doctrine with a deterministic explanatory scheme. The doctrinal theories not only proposed that people sin because they are sinners, but attempted to account for this propensity through a causal relation of Adam to the race. By seeking an answer in terms of the race's relation to Adam, the tradition converted the descriptive generality of "original sin" (we all are sinners like Adam) into some kind of causal necessity (we are all sinners because of what Adam did). Vigilius observes that the point of contention is whether the particular individual participates in inherited sin through his relation to Adam or through his primitive relation to sin (CA, 26).

In one way or another, the various theological traditions had invented causal theories to explain how Adam was responsible for the corruption and guilt of every subsequent individual. Vigilius expresses dissatisfaction with all the theories. He rejects the attempts to interpret Adam as the head of the race by nature, by generation, or by covenant, thereby attacking the real universal, seminal identity, biological descendant, and legal representative theories. He singles out the federal theology as a particularly ridiculous construct, condemning it as "historical-fantastic" (CA, 25). The rejection of any ontic, biological, or legal solidarity with Adam means that the immediate imputation of Adam's guilt is out of the question. Neither is Vigilius interested in any causal transmission of Adam's corruption. For him, the Scholastic alternatives of the debility of original sin as the loss of the *donum supernaturalis* or as concupiscence are equally misguided. Vigilius even criticizes Lutheranism's tendency to use the biological motif to explain the presence of corruption and guilt in the individual (CA, 57). The problem is not the inadequacy of the particular theories presented in the textbooks, but the folly of trying to glean understanding from any theory at all. In his journals Kierkegaard ironically remarks, "To say that the church teaches original sin, that the Catholic church teaches it thus and the Protestant church thus, to erect a speculative concept which explains original sin and sin at all—this is indeed the task of the learned and the wise in our time. The more concrete understanding of it in the individual, that is to say, the way I have to understand it, is a simpler, less complicated task, which I have chosen" (JP, 2:1248).

According to Kierkegaard, the attempts to explain original sin through the relation of the individual to the sin of Adam has two unfortunate consequences. First, dogmatics itself commits the sin he had feared psychology would commit: it subjects the individual's sin to a deterministic explanation and destroys the mood of responsibility. Each theory contains an implicit metaphysical system in which "sin" can be explicated in terms of some supraconcept like "covenant," "real universal," or "biological inheritance." Kierkegaard's attacks upon the Hegelian system apply equally well to the metaphysical systems of the dogmaticians. Rather than a metaphysics of Absolute Spirit, they presuppose a metaphysics of covenant, or organism, or real universals, and use it to relate the sin of Adam to the sin of the individual as cause to effect.

Second, the theories cannot help the individual discern the roots of sinfulness in himself. All of the theories require a fundamental difference between Adam and all subsequent individuals. Vigilius observes, "The error in the preceding is here more evident, for as a result of this Adam is now so fantastically placed outside of history that he is the only one who is excluded from the Atonement" (CA, 28). The chasm between Adam's pre-Fall situation and ours renders him incapable of illuminating our own predicament. For example, in the Scholastic tradition Adam's enjoyment of supernatural rectitude of will and love for God locates him outside the race. Kierkegaard remarks, "The whole doctrine of original sin is presented in the Catholic church as so essentially irrelevant to the single individual that it could be compared best to the outer title page, which is cut off when the book is bound, and for that reason *justitia originalis* (the state of original righteousness) is also so far removed from the person that this is best compared to a splendid binding that bears no relation to the book" (JP, 4:4003). Even the Lutheran focus on Adam's state of perfect felicity in the garden makes the motivation for sin unintelligible. Vigilius remarks, "The more fantastically Adam was arrayed, the more inexplicable became the fact that he could sin" (CA, 36). Such a portrayal of unmotivated perversity cannot help an individual detect the springs of sin in his own soul.

Through these theories, the Augustinian-Lutheran tradition had attempted to address the question "How did I come to be such a sinner?" Although Kierkegaard rejects its strategy of answering in terms of the race's relation to Adam, he does think that the question itself is legitimate. An answer can be given through psychological investigation, if properly pursued. Unlike causal theories, Kierkegaard's psychological descriptions of motivational patterns can be integrated with dogmatics without destroying the essential mood. In order to prevent the free "leap" from collapsing into a determined "state," psychology must be observation rather than speculation about causal schemes. Of course, Haufniensis's observations are guided by the conviction that the self is teleologically oriented to a higher integration. But this perspective only provides a means of organizing his observations; it does not impose a causal psychodynamic theory upon them.

The relationship of dogmatics and psychology is the principle subject of *The Concept of Anxiety*. As the subtitle of the work suggests, *The Concept of Anxiety* is an investigation of a psychological concept that orients the reader in relation to the dogmatic concept of original sin. Although this "anxiety" and original sin are clearly not identical, they seem to have parallel functions, and this is the key to their relationship. Vigilius describes original sin as the "ideal" possibility of sin, while he refers to anxiety as the "actual" possibility of sin (CA, 21). That they share the feature "possibility" suggests that each, in the manner appropriate to its domain of discourse, accounts for the actuality of the same thing. The fundamental issue for Vigilius is the relation of these ideal and actual possibilities. Both somehow "explain" actual sins, but the purposes and logics of their explanations differ significantly.

Dogmatics asks the question "Why do people sin?" and answers, "Because they are sinners." This "ideal" explanation locates the individual sinner in a new conceptual framework. Psychology, on the other hand, asks the question "Why do people sin?" and answers, "People sin because they are anxious." Psychology's real interest is in the expanded question "Why would anyone ever want to sin?" It seeks an answer not by proposing a new conceptual framework, but by exploring human motivations. Accordingly, it searches for some antecedent psychological state that might predispose a person to sin. Vigilius writes, "But this abiding something out of which sin constantly arises . . . this predisposing presupposition, sin's real possibility, is a subject matter of interest for psychology" (CA, 21). Appropriately, the general tone of *The Concept of Anxiety* is one of relentless observation of psychological states. It is significant that Kierkegaard employed the pseudonym "Vigilius Haufniensis" (Watchman of Copenhagen). Vigilius the psychologist does not exhort or edify; he merely scrutinizes human pathos.

Vigilius uses the story of Adam as the archetype of human motivation rather than as a deterministic explanation of the race's sinfulness. The story of Adam is the story of everyone, depicting the paradigmatic situation from which all sin arises. Vigilius first considers the essential features of this "quality" of experience, apart from the differentiating influences of heredity and environment. Only then can the "qualitative" factors affecting the different manifestations of this condition be explored.

The psychologist's concern is Adam's state of innocence, or "dreaming spirit." "Dreaming spirit," psychologically considered, is anxiety, an aspect of all subjectivity. It is not a mere emotional episode, but a pervasive potentiality. It is not a response to a particular object, but a response to all objects apprehended as possibilities for one's own free self-development. Consequently, Kierkegaard could describe anxiety as a state that endures before and after particular overt episodes. Unlike a "stage," anxiety is not chosen by the individual; it comes over him. Anxiety is the passional by-product of the self's development out of its immediate unity with its physical and social environment. In immediacy the affective and somatic dimensions of the individual are indistinguishable. This immediate unity, however, is disturbed by the latent presence of "spirit," the power to separate and reintegrate the "soul" and the body, and the individual and the environment. Spirit is the power of "being able," of actualizing different possibilities, of assuming responsibility for the shape of one's own life. However, this anxiety, generated by the lure of possibility, is an ambivalent or "dialectical" state. In fact, Kierkegaard describes it as "antipathetic sympathy" and "sympathetic antipathy" (CA, 42). The possibility not only attracts but also repels the individual, for immediate unity is secure and comfortable, while the unrealized possibility is unknown and risky. There is simultaneously a motivation to move beyond immediacy, and to remain in it.

Although the ultimate object of anxiety is the self's own responsibility for itself, more "proximate" objects, particular possibilities that the individual encounters or imagines, catalyze it. The situation becomes further complicated when the particular possibility that awakens anxiety is an ethical prohibition. Here two different possibilities each attract and repel the individual. There is motivation to choose the possibility of disobedience, not because it is evil (the innocent individual does not understand "evil" anyway), but because the prospect of "being able" is attractive. On the other hand, the security of immediacy also attracts the individual. Furthermore, the possibility of obedience, of actualizing an ideal, of performing a task, also attracts, while the prospect of the burden of moral responsibility generates a nostalgia for immediacy.

Many commentators have noted that Vigilius does not devote much attention to the possibility of obedience. This attitude has suggested to some that for Kierkegaard the fall into sin is the only real option on the road to spiritual maturity. Perhaps Kierkegaard has inserted a *"felix culpa"* theme into a Hegelian developmental view of spirit in which immediacy can only be overcome through guilt. However, one must remember that Vigilius is only concerned with describing the actual relation between anxiety and sin. Psychology has no business wondering if there could have been a nonsinful maturation from anxiety to fully developed spirit. Even theological speculation about what would have happened had Adam not fallen only distracts from the actual fact of sin. Vigilius writes, "That the time of dogmatics and ethics, as well as one's own time, has often been wasted by pondering what might have happened had Adam not sinned merely proves that one brings along an incorrect mood, and consequently an incorrect concept" (CA, 36). However, in *Concluding Unscientific Postscript*, Climacus does insist that human beings did have the possibility of a nonsinful maturation and have lost it (CUP, 517). This can only be affirmed in a mood of contrition not only for the guilt of lost innocence, but also for a forfeited possibility. In any case, Vigilius is concerned primarily with the attractive and repellent aspect of the possibility of disobedience, because this is the possibility that has been actualized.

It is this ambivalence of anxiety that makes it such a useful explanatory device. In the journals Kierkegaard frequently describes anxiety as the "middle term" of temptation. The "dialectical" motivational dynamics make obedience, disobedience, and nostalgia for immediacy all understandable, without making any of them necessary. This explanation is an improvement upon the "explanation of sin" in the Augustinian-Lutheran tradition. In actual practice, Augustine and the subsequent theologians treated Adam as an instance of abstract *liberum arbitrium*, rejecting communion with God without any obvious motive. The medieval tradition proceeded to regard Adam's descendants as motivated by concupiscence, without explaining the psychological roots of concupiscence. Even the "pride" that the Lutheran tradition attributed to the descendants of Adam invited further psychological analysis. For Kierkegaard, the investigation of anxiety takes the place of speculation about Adam's state of perfection and inherited pride and sensuality. Anxiety has the inestimable advantage of illuminating the roots of an individual's own temptation in a way the traditional formulations could not. Moreover, the psychological investigation could do this without militating against the mood of responsibility.

The analysis of anxiety is the crucial "middle term" that shows how the doctrine of original sin as a rule for regarding the individual is to be applied to the concrete phenomena of an individual's subjective life. For Kierkegaard, the general rule is that each individual should regard his sinful acts as establishing and manifesting his identity, and regard the sinful acts of the race as revealing the truth about himself. The psychological investigation of anxiety shows how the "act establishes identity" force of the doctrine can be applied to passional experience. In general, an individual's past acts are perceived by the individual to betoken future possibilities. Because one has murdered in the past, one imagines that one may do so in the future. Anxiety apprehends the individual's past as its simultaneously repellent and attractive possible future; it is the subjective basis of the relation of the individual's past and future. Kierkegaard insists that each new act should not be thought of as occurring in a vacuum, unconnected with the past acts of the agent. He does not atomize the agent into discrete, unrelated "leaps." On the other hand, Kierkegaard does not unify the agent by appealing to any automatically functioning "habit." One's past does not affect one's future according to any mechanical or organic necessity. Anxiety serves as the main psychological condition, or "middle term," that makes talk about the identity of the agent possible.

Furthermore, anxiety serves as a middle term for talk about the identity of the individual and the race. The theological tradition had attempted to restrict this coinherence of the individual and the race to Adam alone. Vigilius, however, employs "anxiety" to show how the coinherence of the individual and the race can be regarded as a psychological phenomenon in everyone. The race is neither an automatic multiplication of the members of an animal species, nor is it a collection of atomistically separated individuals. Augustinianism, Vigilius fears, undialectically approximates "race" to the instinctive duplication of an animal species. Pelagianism, on the other hand, "does not have the power to spin individuals into the web of the race but lets each individual stick out like the loose ends of a thread" (CA, 186). It "permits every individual to play his little history in his own private theatre unconcerned about the race" (CA, 34). Vigilius insists that the deeds of each individual create new possibilities that alter the race, and the race presents possibilities that define the individual. The deeds of one individual manifest a new potential of human nature to every other individual. Vigilius writes, "Every individual is essentially interested in the history of all other individuals, and just as essentially in his own" (CA, 29).

Once again, "anxiety" is the pivotal middle term. Vigilius remarks, "fine things have been said about this subject [how one individual serves as an "example" to another, revealing to that individual a possibility for his own self]; however, a psychological intermediate term is frequently lacking, namely, the explanation of how it happens that the example has such power" (CA, 75). It is anxiety that apprehends the actuality of others as a possibility for oneself. The story of one sinner is enough to declare that sin is a possibility for the individual. This phenomenon is one of the central motifs of Frater Taciturnus's "Epistle to the Reader" in *Stages on Life's Way*, in which a reformed gambler absolutely identifies with the suicide of an unregenerate gambler whom he knew to be a better person (SLW, 431). Kierkegaard's novel theological move was to use this analysis of "anxiety over the race" as an explanation of the "actual possibility" of the corporate dimension of sin. The analysis demonstrates how the unity in sin that the doctrine describes in regard to agency can motivate the dynamics of the individual's psychic life.

"Anxiety" also serves as a middle term in relation to the historical character of the sinful environment. Vigilius points out that the only real difference between Adam's situation and ours is that we have a "derived" environment. We are born into a familial and cultural situation that has already been shaped by the past sins of the race. The particular past sins of the race form a set of specific possibilities that confront the individual in the present. The individual fears that the specific "sins of the fathers" will recur in his own life. Of course, Vigilius warns, "The greatest degree of quantitative determination no more explains the leap than does the least degree" (CA, 36). The "more or less" of temptation in the environment can be observed by psychology, but, in the context of Christian discourse, has no power to excuse any individual. For Kierkegaard, this history of "quantitative" anxiety serves the same explanatory function that the theory of the biological transmission of corruption served in the Augustinian tradition. It does show how an individual can be affected by the sinfulness of the race's history. However, unlike the biological theory, it does not conflict with the mood of personal responsibility.

In these ways "anxiety" holds together "act" language and "state" language. The individual's past and future, and the individual and the race, are unified by passionate self-concern, not by any organic or mechanical necessity. The possibilities for the self apprehended through anxiety motivate the individual to enact this unity, but they do not "necessitate" it. Individuals are concerned about the relation of their specific pasts and futures, and this anxious concern can lead them to enact a unified life of sin.

In treating the traditional Augustinian-Lutheran doctrine of original sin, Kierkegaard neither reduced its "state" quality to a series of leaps (acts), nor sacrificed its "leap" character to a deterministic explanation of the state. He sought to avoid the atomized individual acts of Pelagianism without absorbing individual acts into a deterministic system. In order to do this, Kierkegaard carefully distinguished the two questions "How is sin related to my identity?" and "How did I come to be a sinner?" The first is a question for dogmatics (the ideal possibility of sinful acts), and the second is a question for psychology (the actual possibility of sinful acts). Because the questions differ, the relationship of "act" and "state" must be examined separately in each one. The dogmatic answer relates acts to states as the establishment and manifestation of a unitary identity, while the psychological answer relates acts to states as the free response to enduring possibilities. "Original sin" gives a unified identity and character description of the individual, while "anxiety" points to the possible motivational sources of this unity. Although "original sin" and "anxiety" are not the same, they are related. The doctrine "orients" psychology by suggesting that there may be a passional basis to the unity of the agent that it describes, and psychology shows how the doctrine can be used not only to describe the agent, but also to illuminate the first stirrings of temptation. Anxiety can become the "middle term" showing how this described unity is forged in the psychic life of the individual. The psychological answer regards sinful acts as a free, but undetermined, response to an enduring passional state. The acts reinforce and qualify the passional state, while the passional state, as a matter of fact, does motivate a homogeneous set of acts. If these two answers get confused, acts of sin may be seen as the manifestation of anxiety (and therefore to be pitied rather than condemned), or acts of sin may be seen as motivated by a sinful identity (and therefore psychologically inexplicable).

Kierkegaard's one complaint with the Augustinian-Lutheran tradition is that it did not appreciate the value of psychology and mistakenly sought the actual possibility of the individual's sin in the identity description of Adam provided by dogma (the ideal possibility). This move forced the theological tradition to resolve the tension between "act" and "state" by attributing the act to Adam and the state to his descendants. The connection between Adam's act and the state of the race then had to be explained through some scheme of cause and effect borrowed from various metaphysical systems. This made the state of subsequent individuals seem predetermined, and it militated against the proper mood of self-ascription of responsibility. By using psychology to explore the actual possibility of sin, Kierkegaard was able to avoid this problem. Psychology, as he used it, described motivations that could possibly, but not necessarily, lead to action. The mood of observation itself could be used by Christianity to promote deepened self-scrutiny and repentance.

III

The Limits of the Ethical in Kierkegaard's The Concept of Anxiety and Kant's Religion within the Limits of Reason Alone

by Ronald M. Green

An individual who turns (or returns) to Kierkegaard's work after prolonged and sympathetic immersion in Kant's ethical writings has an astonishing experience. At first he encounters what seems to be an alien landscape where the familiar Kantian methods and values—the insistence on reason, rational "objectivity," human autonomy, and supremacy of the moral law—have all been replaced by their opposites—paradox, radical subjectivity, revelation, and faith. His disorientation is accentuated by the constant polemic he encounters against rationalistic philosophy and "speculation," a polemic directed principally against Hegel and his followers but seemingly relevant as well to Kant. Yet, as this Kantian "newcomer" settles in, as he examines his surroundings more closely, he finds that beneath the overgrowth of new forms of expression many key features of the older Kantian landscape are present. Indeed, as he looks further, he discovers that not only are many of the larger features of the intellectual terrain similar, but smaller objects—very particular ideas, patterns of organization, and even concrete illustrations—are often identical. And he wonders whether he has discovered a new region or merely stumbled upon the old after the passage of time.

Nowhere is this sense of familiarity experienced more acutely than in reading Kierkegaard's *Concept of Anxiety*. One who has worked with the more provocative and difficult passages of Kant's philosophy of religion—especially book 1 of the *Religion within the Limits of Reason Alone*,[1] where Kant develops his understanding of the "radical evil" of the human will—finds himself immediately at home within the confines of Kierkegaard's penetrating discussion of hereditary sin. Not only are many of Kant's key themes picked up here, but the organization of the two works betrays surprising similarities. True, whole sections of Kierkegaard's discussion are new and contain levels of psychological analysis lacking in Kant. Then, too, some halting suggestions about faith and grace made by Kant are carried by Kierkegaard to conclusions that would have troubled the earlier philosopher. Yet throughout, one has the sense that *The Concept of Anxiety* converses with the *Religion* and, in some senses, represents a natural development of Kant's philosophy of religion. Read together the two treatises even complement one another, with Kant's careful conceptual analysis illuminating Kierkegaard's major unexplained presuppositions and Kierkegaard's psychological insight adding a new dimension to Kant's more formal analysis.

There are several broad parallels between the thinking of Kant and Kierkegaard that should be mentioned at the outset. Recently, some of these parallels have been emphasized by commentators who have challenged the conventional wisdom that places Kierkegaard in sharp discontinuity with the previous rationalist tra-

---

[1]All references are to the translation by Theodore M. Green and Hoyt H. Hudson (New York: Harper & Row, 1960).

dition.[2] These parallels not only provide further evidence for Kierkegaard's possible indebtedness to Kant, but also furnish much of the intellectual background for both Kant's and Kierkegaard's discussions of sin.

Foremost among the features common to Kant and to Kierkegaard is an anthropology that emphasizes human freedom. Both men view the human being as a limited, finite creature pulled by natural "inclinations" and desires, but, nevertheless, possessing the capacity for controlling impulse and desire through a process of free choice. This capacity fundamentally distinguishes man from other creatures; it confers a special "dignity" on *all* who are human (whatever their stations in life[3]); and it renders each individual's existence a perpetual striving toward a higher destiny.

For both of these thinkers, the reality of freedom and the importance of this higher destiny are known through an "imperative" laid upon each person's existence. For Kant, this imperative takes the form of reason's moral law (the categorical imperative), while for Kierkegaard, it is a broader requirement of moral and spiritual development and individuation. Kant and Kierkegaard's understanding of the specific norms bearing upon human life, their respective moral and religious ideals, are not identical. Indeed, it has been argued that they are fundamentally different—that Kant's a prioristic, formalistic moral law differs from Kierkegaard's understanding of the normative pattern for the religious individual.[4] I am not convinced that this is true. Individual self-development plays a far more important role in Kant's thinking than is com-

---

[2]See, for example, Robert L. Perkins, "For Sanity's Sake: Kant, Kierkegaard, and Father Abraham," in *Kierkegaard's Fear and Trembling: Critical Appraisals*, ed. Robert L. Perkins (University AL; University of Alabama Press, 1981) 43-61; also, Jerry H. Gill, "Kantianism," in *Kierkegaard and Great Traditions*, ed. Niels Thulstrup and Marie M. Thulstrup (Copenhagen: C. A. Reitzels Boghandel, 1981) 223-29.

[3]Compare Kant's affirmation of universal human dignity in the *Foundations of the Metaphysics of Morals*, trans. Lewis White Beck (Indianapolis: Bobbs Merrill, 1959) 53f. (Preussiche Akademie der Wissenschaft edition, 4:435f.) with Kierkegaard's remarks in EO, 2:181, 280.

[4]This is the contention of George J. Stack in his *Kierkegaard's Existential Ethics* (University AL: University of Alabama Press, 1977) 169f.

monly recognized (as evidenced, for example, by his stress in *The Metaphysics of Morals* and the *Lectures on Ethics* on the priority of duties to oneself).[5] There are also points in Kierkegaard's writings where he displays an appreciation very similar to Kant's of the basic minimal rules of social interaction (which Kierkegaard terms the "negative" duties and Kant the "perfect" duties).[6] Important as this matter is, however, in both men's treatment of the problem of sin, the precise content of their respective ideals is less important than their view of the ideal as a demanding challenge before which every individual is likely to fall short.

In addition to agreeing about this sense of requirement, both Kant and Kierkegaard believe that responsibility extends to the exercise of one's will, not to the actual consequences generated by one's choice. Both also seem to agree, however, that in willing, one's responsibility encompasses the *likely* consequences of one's acts. Neither thinker, in other words, appears to advocate a position of benevolent dispositions combined with an attitude of "consequences be damned." In fact, it is the rigor of this requirement imposed upon the will, a responsibility for attending to every *remotely foreseeable* consequence of one's choice, that partly shapes each thinker's perception of the stringency of the moral demand.[7] Nevertheless, in the last analysis it is for the informed exercise of one's will alone that one is morally called to account. This accountability means that for both Kant and Kierkegaard, the forum of moral judgment is essentially internal. Both view moral judgment as first of all an act engaged in by the self against the self. No outer human court is more capable or more demanding than the forum of conscience, and because of the nature of moral judgment, only

---

[5] *The Doctrine of Virtue, Part II of the Metaphysics of Morals*, trans. Mary J. Gregor (Philadelphia: University of Pennsylvania Press, 1964) part 1, and *Lectures on Ethics*, trans. Louis Infield (New York: Harper & Row, 1963) 116ff.

[6] Compare, for example, Kant's distinction between "perfect" and "imperfect" duties in *The Doctrine of Virtue* and between "obligatory" and "meritorious" duties in the *Foundations*, 47f. (Akademie edition, 4:429f.) with Kierkegaard's classification of the duties in EO, 2:267f.

[7] A view of this sort appears to be given especially sharp expression by Kierkegaard in Quidam's Diary (SLW, 348).

God (who sees the heart) shares with the self the role as one's accuser and judge.

Mention of God as surveyor of the inner moral life points to a final broad parallel between the thinking of Kant and Kierkegaard: their shared belief that morality must find its grounding in religious faith. Those whose familiarity with Kant is limited to *The Foundations of the Metaphysics of Morals*, with its insistence on human autonomy in ethics and its sharp criticism of religious "heteronomy," will find this emphasis on faith markedly un-Kantian. But it is the point of Kant's subsequent writings on the philosophy of religion that religious belief is needed to provide rational coherence for the moral exercise of the will. Kant goes so far as to declare that without faith in a moral God, the moral law itself would become vain and imaginary.[8] Kant's detailed argumentation here is sometimes called the moral "proof" of God's existence, but it is less a proof than a rigorous exploration of the logical preconditions of rational moral commitment.[9] For Kant, religious faith derives not from idle speculative interests but from an urgent choice made in the sphere of moral life. In this respect, for Kant, no less than for Kierkegaard, faith involves an act of will and a leap. It follows from commitment to the moral life. And it is a choice made in defiance of what worldly "wisdom" and experience tell us—for in the world, moral order and moral commitment find little support. It is also a choice always marked by uncertainty. Kierkegaard's existence lived over a depth of "70,000" fathoms (CUP, 126) has a counterpart in Kant's "wavering" rational faith. For both thinkers, therefore, faith stands in a different epistemological category than knowledge. It always lacks certainty, but far from being a reason for regret, faith's objective uncertainty for both thinkers is a cause for celebration. As a result of its uncertainty, faith becomes not a lethargic and

---

[8]*Critique of Practical Reason*, 118 (Akademie edition, 4:114). See also *The Critique of Teleological Judgment*, trans. James C. Meredith (Oxford: Clarendon Press, 1928) 120f. (Akademie edition, 5:452).

[9]For a fuller discussion of the logic of Kant's argument, see my *Religious Reason* (New York: Oxford University Press, 1978) chs. 1-3.

fearful response to God's overwhelming power or presence, but a free and courageous act.[10]

It should be clear, then, that many basic tenets of Kierkegaard's thinking are at least prefigured in Kant's work. Of course, there seem to be important differences as well. For all his interest in religion, for example, Kant would limit religious faith and speculation to a zone sternly ruled by morality. In Kant's view, morality always remains supreme and religion is its servant. It follows from this view that for Kant there are no direct duties to God. Full religious obedience can be accomplished by the performance of one's duties to oneself and to one's neighbor, and a religious belief that, in the name of divine service, contravened morality would be denounced by Kant as a form of "heteronomy." Futhermore, since Kant believed that all the religious beliefs required for moral commitment are freely furnished by one's own reason, revelation and historical faith are for him "in principle" unnecessary.[11] This means concretely that for Kant, Abraham is not the "father of faith," as he is for Kierkegaard, but is a scandalous fanatic best forgotten.

As striking as these contrasts seem to be, they serve in a peculiar way as a fitting introduction to the specific parallels to be discussed here between Kant's *Religion* and Kierkegaard's *Concept of Anxiety*. It is in the *Religion* that these two themes that later are to preoccupy Kierkegaard so much receive explicit attention. It is here that Kant discusses extensively the matter of duties to God and concludes that there are "no special duties" of this sort distinguishable from one's duties to self and to neighbor.[12] And it is here that Kant first broaches the matter of Abraham's sacrifice of Isaac, contending that no command in violation of morality may be obeyed.[13] Because of the centrality of these themes in the *Religion* it is reasonable to suppose that if Kierkegaard is not in agreement

---

[10]Compare Kant's concluding remarks in the *Critique of Practical Reason*, 152f. (Akademie edition, 5:146f.) with Kierkegaard's comments in CUP, 182, 381f.

[11]Perkins, "For Sanity's Sake," 52.

[12]*Religion*, 142.

[13]Ibid., 91n, 175; Kant deals similarly with Abraham in *The Conflict of the Faculties*, trans. Mary J. Gregor (New York: Abaris Books, 1979) 115n.

with Kant on these points he may be involved in dialogue with him. If one further bears in mind the possibility that Kierkegaard's *Fear and Trembling*, where both the idea of direct duties to God and Abraham's obedience are defended, may be not so much a discussion of heteronomous religious morality as an anguished treatment of the problem of repentance (FT, 108f.), then even the disagreement between Kant and Kierkegaard on these matters may be less dramatic than it first appears. As I shall show, Kant also recognized that repentance is the most fearful challenge to our ordinary notion of justice.

With this background, one might now turn to the specific correspondences between the *Religion* and *The Concept of Anxiety*. In particular, four major points deserve mention. They are: (1) the ideality of ethics and the absoluteness of the moral command; (2) the "inexplicability" of sin despite its relationship to human nature; (3) Adam as Everyman through whose sin all humans become corrupt; and (4) the problematic nature of repentance and the necessary role of faith and grace in the economy of redemption.

The Ideality of Ethics

In the introduction to *The Concept of Anxiety*, Kierkegaard seeks to explain why he will devote so much attention to the notion of hereditary sin. He does so by maintaining that with the appearance of sin, "all is lost for ethics" (CA, 19). Because the idea of hereditary sin denies the claim that virtue can be realized, it expresses in *dogmatic* form what ethics knows the moment that sin comes forth: that sin and ethics are radically incompatible and that ethics must be "shipwrecked" on sin's appearance.

Behind this strong statement of ethics' incompatibility with sin is a further idea: that ethics is an "ideal" science. "Ethics," says Kierkegaard, "points to ideality as a task and assumes that every man possesses the requisite conditions" (CA, 16). For this reason, ethics will have nothing to do with the idea that an individual cannot meet its demands or that he can only partly do so. Ethics is, and should be, uncompromising in what it requires.

The more ideal ethics is, the better. It must not permit itself to be

> distracted by the babble that it is useless to require the impossible.
> For even to listen to such talk is unethical and is something for
> which ethics has neither *time* nor *opportunity*. Ethics will have
> nothing to do with bargaining. (CA, 17)

It is this understanding of ethics' ideality, then, that underlies
Kierkegaard's view of sin. Without this ideality, sin would not be
the fundamental challenge to ethics that it is, nor would it need to
be transcended in religion. But why does Kierkegaard insist that
ethics—as the normative "science" bearing on human life—has this
ideal character? At least on the surface, this view appears unrea-
sonable. After all, no one is entirely good. We all occasionally fail
to perform the moral duties we know are incumbent upon us, but
we do not from that conclude that we are "unethical." Nor do we
seem to believe that moral judgment requires unerring excellence
or that it casts a wholly negative light on partial moral efforts. Yet
this is just what Kierkegaard seems to be saying. In a passage of
the *Postscript*, he forcefully expresses this view.

> It is possible to *be both* good and bad, as we say quite simply,
> that a man has tendencies to both good and evil. But it is impos-
> sible *at one and the same time to become both good and bad.* Aestheti-
> cally the requirement has been imposed on the poet not to present
> these abstract patterns of virtue, or satanic incarnations of evil, but
> to follow Goethe's example and give us characters which are both
> good and bad. And why is this a legitimate demand? Because the
> poet is supposed to describe human beings as they *are,* and every
> human being is *both good and bad;* and because the medium of the
> poet is imagination, is *being* but not *becoming,* or at most becoming
> in a very much foreshortened perspective. But take the individual
> out of the medium of the imagination, the medium of being, and
> place him in existence: Ethics will at once demand that he be
> pleased to become, and then he becomes—either good or bad. . . .
> This *summa summarum,* that all men *are* both good and bad, does
> not concern Ethics in the least. For Ethics does not have the me-
> dium of *being,* but the medium of *becoming.* (CUP, 376f.)

Kierkegaard's point here is poetically expressed. His distinction between *being* and *becoming* suggests a more basic distinction
between what the lived reality of a person's life has been and what
that person *wills* to make himself in the present moment of moral
decision. But beyond this, Kierkegaard is not clear. Why does a

single moment of willing determine the moral value of a whole course of life? And why is that willing either good or bad? Can there not be an "intermediate" kind of willing, a qualified willing that is less than perfect but that is not immoral?

Kierkegaard does not answer these questions. But Kant discusses them in the *Religion*. Here, too, as a preamble to a discussion of sin, one finds an insistence on the ideality of ethics. But Kant's treatment of this issue—especially when connected with some of his earlier discussion in the *Foundations of the Metaphysics of Morals* and the *Critique of Practical Reason*—helps clarify what Kierkegaard only presumes.

Kant begins his remarks with the question of whether by nature man is good or evil. Very much like Kierkegaard, he considers at the outset the possibility that such absolute evaluations may be inappropriate.

> The conflict between the two hypotheses . . . is based on a disjunctive proposition: *Man is* (by nature) *either morally good or morally evil.* It might occur to any one, however, to ask whether this disjunction is valid, and whether some might not assert that man is by nature neither of the two, others, that man is at once both, in some respects good, in other respects evil. Experience actually seems to substantiate the middle ground between the two extremes.

But almost as soon as he raises this possibility, Kant dismisses it.

> It is however, of great consequence to ethics in general to avoid admitting, so long as it is possible, of anything morally intermediate, whether in actions (*adiophora*) [*sic*] or in human characters; for with such ambiguity all maxims are in danger of forfeiting their precision and stability.[14]

Here, then, is the very ideality that Kierkegaard assumes. But why does Kant hold what he himself concedes is a "rigoristic" view?[15] Why not a less precise and more ambiguous "intermediate" position? The roots of the answer to this lie in Kant's basic ethical theory. The morally good person, for Kant, is one whose will

---

[14]*Religion*, 17f.

[15]Ibid.

is determined not by self love (Kant's very general term for private or particular interests of any sort), but by duty. Duty, in turn, is the dictate of the categorical imperative, that formal principle requiring all maxims (all proposed general rules of conduct; all policies one has set for oneself) to be capable of being willed at the same time as universal law.[16] The morally good person, therefore, is one who chooses to establish this imperative as the supreme guide to his or her conduct. Of course, one need not do this. One can will *never* to obey the categorical imperative (something Kant views as humanly impossible).[17] Or one can will *sometimes*—even in most cases—to obey this imperative, but on occasion to retain the option of not obeying.

This last position would seem to be an intermediate one between good and evil. However, as Kant points out in the second *Critique* and the *Religion*, it really is not intermediate at all. For, a rational person who wills *on occasion* not to obey the moral law must have some higher general principle that determines what he shall do in each instance of choice. But what could this principle be but the principle of "self love" or private interest? The maxim of the individual who wills occasional obedience to the moral law is one to the effect that he will obey this law *unless* it proves too onerous for him to do so. Since his final referent is to what is convenient to him, this individual allows self-interest to become the arbiter of what he shall do, and he stands with those who make self-interest the first consideration of their will. There is, therefore, no intermediate position between unqualified obedience to the moral law and disobedience. In the clear-sightedness of honest moral analysis, one either is moral or is not. In characteristically difficult terms, Kant spells this out in his discussion in the *Religion*.

> [T]he answer to the question at issue [whether man is by nature good or evil] rests upon the observation, of great importance to morality, that freedom of the will is of a wholly unique nature in that an incentive can determine the will to an action *only in so far*

---

[16]This imperative is usually taken to imply the requirement that maxims be universalizable. For a different interpretation, one stressing the universal *acceptability* of maxims, see my *Religious Reason*, ch. 1.

[17]*Religion*, 30.

as the individual has incorporated it into his maxim (has made it the general rule in accordance with which he will conduct himself); only thus can an incentive, whatever it may be, co-exist with the absolute spontaneity of the will (i.e. freedom). But the moral law, in the judgment of reason, is in itself an incentive, and whoever makes it his maxim is *morally* good. If, now this law does not determine a person's will in the case of an action which has reference to the law, an incentive contrary to it must influence his choice; and since, by hypothesis, this can only happen when a man adopts this incentive (and thereby the deviation from the moral law) into his maxim (in which case he is an evil man) it follows that his disposition in respect to the moral law is never indifferent, neither good nor evil.

Neither can a man be morally good in some ways and at the same time morally evil in others. His being good in one way means that he has incorporated the moral law into his maxim; were he, therefore, at the same time evil in another way, while his maxim would be universal as based on the moral law of obedience to duty, which is essentially single and universal, it would at the same time be only particular; but this is a contradiction.[18]

The insistence on ethics' ideality is not, therefore, just a matter of private moral preferences, nor is it a matter of poetic exaggeration introduced by Kierkegaard to shape his case against ethics. Kant's more formal analysis helps sustain what both he and Kierkegaard assume. (This analysis, incidentally, seems to me not to be a philosopher's abstraction. It has powerful human significance. In the wake of the wars and mass persecutions of this century, we have perhaps learned that those who make only qualified moral commitments ["I will be moral unless . . ."] often behave no differently in the crisis of choice than those who are openly wicked. As Kant saw, a contingent commitment to moral duty can often be the same as no commitment at all.)

The "Inexplicability" of Sin
Despite Its Relationship to Human Nature

This understanding of the ideality of ethics furnishes one part of the structure of thought that leads both Kant and Kierkegaard

---

[18]Ibid., 19f.

back to an appreciation of the religious idea of original sin. Another major component in that structure, however, is their view of human nature. For both Kant and Kierkegaard, man's nature makes sin possible. At the same time, it in no way requires or "causes" man to sin. In fact, both thinkers absolutely repudiate any effort to provide a causal explanation of sin, and both strongly affirm sin's origination in an inherently "inexplicable" act of human freedom.

I have already indicated that Kant and Kierkegaard share an anthropological perspective that sees man as a composite of finitude and transcendence (freedom). For Kierkegaard, sin has its beginning when the self, rendered "dizzy" by the possibility of freedom, finds itself "laying hold of finitude to support itself " (CA, 61). While Kant's discussion of sin lacks the psychological dimensions of Kierkegaard's, his moral analysis reveals a broadly similar dynamic. Man is a creature subject to two major "predispositions," Kant tells us. One is the moral predisposition that, if no other incentive worked in opposition to it, would direct the will. But man also has a "natural" predisposition arising from his sensuous nature, the drives and desires he possesses as a finite living being. Were he to subordinate these sensuous impulses to the moral law, he would be virtuous. But in the instant of choice, man somehow inverts the order of priorities. He reaches for the objectives of finitude, and the result is moral evil or sin.

Why does the individual characteristically choose in this fashion? Kant takes pains throughout his discussion in the *Religion* to point out that man's sensuous nature is not to blame. In agreement with the classical Christian tradition—and with Kierkegaard (CA, 27, 79; EO, 2:50)—he maintains that the problem lies not in man's sensuous nature but in his will. To think otherwise would deny to man both freedom and culpability.[19] Furthermore, Kant repeatedly insists that man's sensuous desires also form the material with which reason's formal moral imperative must work. The virtuous human being is not one *without* desires—for that would be no human being at all—but is rather the individual who subjects whatever desires he has to the constant regulation of the moral

---

[19]Ibid.

law. Man's sensuous nature, therefore, though it provides an occasion for both good and evil, is not the source of evil, in Kant's view.[20] Kant would surely agree with Kierkegaard that moral evil stems not from one part of the synthesis that is man, but from "a misrelation in a relation of a synthesis that relates itself to itself" (SUD, 15).

Because he refused to view moral struggle simply as a war between reason and desire, Kant clearly recognized the *rational* possibility of the choice for immorality. In the *Critique of Practical Reason*[21] and again in the *Religion*,[22] Kant repeatedly rejects the Greek view that wrongdoing is folly—the overcoming of reason by desire. A human being's reason can be exercised coherently either in a moral or a selfish fashion, Kant believes. No argument to the effect that immoral willing is imply irrational is convincing.[23] Just as natural causes do not require an individual to sin, neither does reason require him to be moral. Kant thus fully perceived and appreciated the depths of human freedom in this regard.

But Kant will not go beyond observing the possibility of sin. He deliberately refuses to give an answer to the question of why an individual should choose the path of immorality. And in this respect, Kierkegaard appears to follow him. Indeed, this refusal to provide an *explanation* of sin is one of the most striking parallels between the *Religion* and the *Concept of Anxiety*. In Kierkegaard's words, sin admits no explanation: "To want to give a logical explanation of the coming of sin into the world," says Kierkegaard, "is a stupidity that only can occur to people who are comically worried about finding an explanation" (CA, 50). Sin cannot be explained, he insists because it rests on freedom and like any free act in its very concept it resists antecedent explanation. Sin must thus be thought of as entering the world in a qualitative leap (CA, 48, 111), with the "suddenness of the enigmatic" (CA, 30).

---

[20]Ibid., 27, 30, 51.

[21]Ibid., 115f., 120f. (Akademie edition, 5:111f., 115f.).

[22]Ibid., 50.

[23]Ibid.

Kant's agreement here is complete. He resists the effort to explain sin in terms of any "determination" or causation of the will by the natural impulses. Moral evil stems not from these impulses but from a *choice* on our part to allow them sway over the dictates of the moral law. But because this choice rests on freedom, on the reality of our nondetermination by natural causes, it defies any kind of causal explanation and its "ground" or basis must remain forever inscrutable to us. The effort to discover an "explanation" further back beyond the brute fact of a free choice on our part must always re-encounter the mystery of freedom.

> That the ultimate subjective ground of the adoption of moral maxims is inscrutable to us is already evident from this, that since this adoption is free its ground (why, for example, I have chosen evil and not a good maxim) must not be sought in my natural impulses, but always again in a maxim. Now since this maxim also must have its ground, and since apart from maxims no *determining* ground of free choice can or ought to be adduced, we are referred back endlessly in a series of subjective determining grounds without ever being able to reach the ultimate ground.[24]

Adam as Everyman
through Whose Sin We Become Corrupt

Our inability to explain sin means, of course, that wrongdoing is not "necessary." For Kant and for Kierkegaard, sin is sin: imputable wrongdoing and wrongwilling—evil that can and should be avoided. Man's total situation (his natural desires, his finitude, and the ought that bears down on his life) may explain why sin is possible, but it never requires sin. Each human being is constitutionally able to live his life in a proper way without sin. But no one does. For both Kant and Kierkegaard, the misuse of freedom is a universal fact. Not only is every individual guilty of sin—and the most guilty are those who deny this fact—but this sin is profound, enduring, and seemingly inescapable. As has just been seen, the fact of sin cannot be explained. But sin's omnipresence, its persis-

---

[24]Ibid., 17n.

tence, and man's bondage to it are staples of the Christian understanding of Biblical faith. In another remarkably similar move at this
point in their discussions, both Kant and Kierkegaard turn for
deeper insight to the Genesis account of Adam's fall.

The discussions of Adam in the *Religion* and in *The Concept of
Anxiety* both begin with the assertion that man's fall cannot be
viewed as a singular historical occurrence that subsequently in-
fects all men or causally brings about future sin. Kierkegaard is
emphatic on this point. To explain hereditary sin through every
man's relationship to Adam and not through the individual's
"primitive" relationship to sin, he says, is to place Adam fantastically outside history and outside the human race (CA, 26-28). Hereditary sin would then be something present, but Adam would
be "the only one in whom it was not found." This interpretation,
Kierkegaard maintains, confuses everything. If Adam's sin has any
meaning at all, if all humans somehow participate in that sin, a different explanation must be sought. It is to be found, Kierkegaard
argues, in the fact that Adam's sin, the first sin, is "something different than *a* sin, (i.e., a sin like many others)" and "something
different from *one* sin (i.e. no. 1 in relation to no. 2)" (CA, 30). No,
it is the first sin because it "constitutes the nature of the quality:
the first sin is the sin" (CA, 30). In this sense, Adam's sin is not
directly causative but is rather prototypical and representative:
Adam is at once "himself and the race," Kierkegaard continues, and
"that which explains Adam also explains the race and vice versa."
Developing this point, Kierkegaard suggests that in Adam's experience we see truths that are daily reaffirmed in each of our lives.
These include the truth that sin presupposes itself, that nothing
"causes" sin but sin, and that sin enters the world suddenly by a
leap (CA, 32). Similarly confirmed is the claim that through Adam's *first* sin, sin entered the world. "Precisely in the same way,"
says Kierkegaard, "it is true of every man's first sin that through it
sin comes into the world" (CA, 31).

With respect to Adam, Kant almost merely assumes what Kierkegaard feels compelled to argue for at length. Since Kant's basic
endeavor in the *Religion* is to demonstrate the rational, moral significance of key tenets of biblical faith, there is never a question for
him of interpreting original sin literally as a corruption handed

down from our common ancestor. He quickly brushes aside this idea as "inept"[25] and then turns to a view of Adam as prototypical human being and to the Genesis story as a "representation" of fundamental moral truths. Of Adam he says, "*Mutato nomine de ta fabula narratur*" ("change but the name, of you the tale is told"),[26] a remark reminiscent of Kierkegaard's *unum noris omnes* ("if you know one, you know all") (CA, 79).

The Genesis story of Adam's transgression conveys for Kant enduring moral truth. In the narrative of the Fall, for example, is conveyed the understanding that in the search for the origin of evil actions, "every such action must be regarded as though the individual had fallen into it directly from a state of innocence."[27] This view is necessary because "whatever natural causes may be influencing him, . . . his action is yet free and determined by none of these causes; hence it can and must always be judged as an *original* use of his will."[28] This understanding, he adds, agrees very well with the Genesis account, for there evil does not start from a propensity but as a free transgression of the divine command. Kant does not use the words, but his point is very similar to Kierkegaard's: sin presupposes itself.

Kierkegaard's individualized interpretation of Adam's "first" sin as the cause of sin—his claim that sin comes into the world through *every man's* first sin—also has powerful resonance in Kant's discussion. Like Kierkegaard, Kant individualizes the historical element in accounts of Adam's fall and contends that its significance is to be found in the fact that every one of our own transgressions has a quality of pointing backward to a previous time in our lives and a previous transgression. As we trace this sequence backward, we find sin commencing in the very earliest exercise of our will.[29]

---

[25]Ibid., 35.

[26]Ibid., 37.

[27]Ibid., 36.

[28]Ibid.

[29]Ibid., 38.

This "individualized" interpretation of the "first" sin is important, not just because it seems to be shared in part by Kant and Kierkegaard, but because it may also help to explain a far deeper correspondence between the two men: their conviction of the truth of the Christian understanding of man's total and seemingly inescapable bondage to sin. Neither thinker, of course, will accept a purely historical explanation of this understanding. For Kant, in particular, it is preposterous to predicate sin of the species in such a way that it becomes part of human inherited constitution, for that would be contrary to the very idea of freedom. Sin would no longer be sin. Yet Kant does develop an understanding of the "first" sin such that it becomes for each person a cause of virtually inescapable bondage to sin and of total, limitless guilt. Although there is no direct parallel to Kant's analysis in *The Concept of Anxiety*, Kierkegaard does share Kant's conclusions here, and this may be one of those points where Kierkegaard stands in unacknowledged debt to his predecessor, who has managed to refurbish a difficult dogmatic conception.

Two major considerations underlie Kant's discussion of the virtual inescapability of sin. One has already been touched on: the ideality of the moral command, the requirement that to be morally good an individual must will unwavering obedience to the dictates of duty. The second consideration is that no individual is in a position to certify (to himself or to others) that he is morally good. This kind of positive self-evaluation would require the individual to affirm that he has resolved *always* to obey the moral law. Such resolve must be genuine; not a passing whim, but a genuine inner conviction buttressed by a consistent pattern of moral willing.

But can any individual so positively evaluate his will when he subjects it to an honest and searching scrutiny? Kant thinks not, and he identifies three deeply interrelated reasons why this is so. First, there is the problem that even the seemingly firmest present resolve is not yet equivalent to a righteous course of life.[30] Knowing what he does about himself and about human beings generally, the well-intentioned individual must naturally be reluctant to

---

[30]Ibid., 60.

base a globally positive self-estimate on a single moment of willing, when what is required for virtue is a *life* of such willing. A second problem exacerbates the first: the notorious changeableness of the human will. In view of the will's fickleness, what gives an individual the confidence to believe that his present resolve will hold? Kant maintains that while it may seem morbid to dwell on this inconstancy, it is the honest and morally responsible thing to do. Better to approach one's self-justification with "fear and trembling," he contends, than to hold, as we are all prone to do, an exceedingly good opinion of oneself.[31]

Finally, there is the weightiest problem of all: the enormous and seemingly insuperable burden of one's *past* defections from the moral law—even the burden of that single "first" sin in the remote beginnings of the use of one's will.[32] As we survey our past, Kant suggests, each of us can identify moments when we knowingly and freely subverted the priority of duty or where we are at least uncertain as to which motive took precedence in our choice. Past moments of this sort, however, cast a dark shadow on our present and our future. In part, this is the problem of making amends for these previous wrongs—the problem of repentance. But there is also the problem of what these acts say about the very character of our will. If these acts had not been free, if they had been conditioned by forces beyond our control or if they had been shaped by ignorance, we could presumably put them behind us and embark upon our present life of free, moral choice. But if we freely and knowingly made vicious choices in the past, what conceivably can prevent us from doing so again? Precisely because they are free, moral choices thus have a "timeless" quality. One act has enduring significance as a measure of how we use our will, and one past act remains a persistent, recurrent possibility for the future.

All these considerations lead Kant to conclude that every honest person must properly regard himself as morally deficient. Indeed, scrupulous inward self-examination that will not content itself with mere outward show or partial success, and the stern

---

[31]Ibid., 62.

[32]Ibid., 65.

ideality of the law that recognizes no intermediate between good and vicious willing—these combine to point to the conclusion that we are all possessed of a radically evil will. Moreover, since this evil traces back to the first or original exercise of our wills, it is properly thought of as a form of original sin. Kant expresses this conclusion in a passage where he tries to connect his analysis to the insights of biblical and Christian faith:

> This debt which is original, or prior to all the good a man may do— this, and no more, is what we referred to in Book One as the *radical evil in man*—this debt can never be discharged by another person, so far as we can judge according to the justice of our human reason. . . . Now this moral evil (transgression of the moral law, called SIN when the law is regarded *as a divine command*) brings with it endless violations of the law and so *infinite* guilt. The extent of this guilt is due not so much to the *infinitude* of the Supreme Lawgiver whose authority is thereby violated . . . as to the fact that this moral evil lies in the *disposition* and the maxims in general, in *universal basic principles* rather than in particular transgressions. (The case is different before a human court of justice, for such a court attends merely to single offenses and therefore to the deed itself and what is relative thereto, and not to the general disposition.) It would seem to follow, then, that because of the infinite guilt all mankind must look forward to *endless punishment* and exclusion from the kingdom of God.[33]

It needs hardly be said how thoroughly Kierkegaard agrees with Kant at this point. Indeed, a passage in *The Concept of Anxiety* expresses these ideas in terms so similar to Kant's that they suggest direct borrowing.

> Whoever learns to know his guilt only from the finite is lost in the finite, and finitely the question of whether a man is guilty cannot be determined except in an external, juridical and most imperfect sense. Whoever learns to know his guilt only by analogy to judgments of the police court and supreme court never really understands that he is guilty, for if a man is guilty, he is infinitely guilty. (CA, 161)

---

[33]Ibid., 66.

The Problematic Nature of Repentance
and the Role of Faith and Grace in the Economy of Redemption

The course of Kant's analysis takes him to the familiar impasse identified by Christian theology: the seeming embeddedness of sin in human nature. Quite unexpectedly for an Enlightenment thinker, Kant has shown the enormous difficulty of becoming a virtuous person. A rationalist, he has shown the limits and difficulties of rationalism. But Kant does not stop there. He seeks to point a way out of the deep trough of iniquity he has discovered. That path lies through repentance, a topic to which Kant gives considerable attention in the *Religion*. Kant's position here is that it is possible for humans to exercise their will to repent and by so doing to put sin behind them as they embark on a new, upright moral life. In this respect, his position would seem to differ from Kierkegaard's. While Kierkegaard's understanding of repentance is not always clear, it seems to be his principal view that repentance does not alleviate but only sharpens the problem of sin. Repentance, he says repeatedly, is at once the "highest ethical expression" but also "the deepest ethical contradiction" (CA, 117; FT, 108). This characterization seems to be true, on the one hand, because repentance is a distraction from moral conduct. On the other hand, repentance, even if ethically allowable, is impotent before sin: "repentance cannot annul sin; it can only sorrow over it" (CA, 115; FT, 109). For these and other reasons, full redemption depends upon a direct relationship with God and is the product of faith and grace.

Before one concludes that there is complete disagreement between these two thinkers on this point, one must look more closely at Kant's discussion of repentance. In doing so, I think one can see that because of the great honesty and penetration of his analysis, Kant partly subverts his own point. Rather than demonstrating that repentance is a remedy for sin, Kant shows almost the reverse: that repentance is powerless before sin and antagonistic to some key requirements of ethics. In this respect, a careful reading of his discussion must have been enormously instructive to a thinker like

Kierkegaard, who doubts man's ability to effect his own redemption through moral striving. Kierkegaard's repeated allusions to repentance as the "shipwreck" of ethics, in other words, find solid, if unintended, support within Kant's careful discussion in the *Religion*.

The problem that forms Kant's point of departure for his treatment of repentance is that past sins cannot morally be escaped. Each person knows, says Kant, that whatever he may have done in the way of adopting a good disposition, *"he nevertheless started from evil* and this debt he can by no possibility wipe out."[34] Several different problems follow from this one. First, a person "cannot regard the fact that he incurs no new debts subsequent to his change of heart as equivalent to having discharged the old ones." These prior deeds remain, in Kant's view, an offense that somehow must be offset. Second, no one is able through future conduct to produce a surplus to repay these debts "for it is always his duty to do all the good that lies in his power."[35]

How, then, can a person make amends? Part of the answer, says Kant, lies in viewing the suffering created in and through genuine repentance as a suitable punishment for these previous wrongs. But this view produces a new and still more serious problem. In the change of heart effected by repentance, a person's former self—the person who performed these wicked deeds—has vanished. He has been replaced by a "new person" who wills only upright conduct. How, in justice, can punishment be inflicted on the new self who in reality is morally "another person"?

Kant's answer is as complex as the problem. Since the infliction of punishment can be conceived as taking place *"neither before nor after* the change of heart, and is yet necessary," he says, "we must think of it as carried out *during* the change of heart itself and adapted thereto."[36] Just recompense thus becomes for the repentant the profound sorrow over previous sin experienced during repentance and a humble willingness at that moment to accept all

---

[34]Ibid.

[35]Ibid.

[36]Ibid., 67.

future suffering in life, which, though properly not due his changed person, he nevertheless takes upon himself.[37]

Despite its penetration, Kant's solution to the problem of sin—his view of the adequacy of repentance—is not entirely persuasive. One serious difficulty is how one person's suffering can be taken in repayment of another's moral debt. Even if one concedes that a new moral self can somehow repay the previous self's wrong (an issue tangled in notions of retributive punishment), can suffering justly be inflicted on an "innocent" person? If a person has really repented, it may be that he can view his remorse *during* this change as justified punishment for his other, immoral self (who, for a confused instant, he continues to be). But is it not wrong that he should have to suffer subsequent penalties, as Kant claims? Such suffering inflicted on a good person violates one's sense of justice, and the very idea may cause us to resist the full dynamic of repentance that Kant believes must take place. We are thus led to a kind of wrathful anger at repentance and a hardening in sin of the sort that Kierkegaard explores (CA, 116). More serious, however, is the problem of whether *any* self-established and self-accepted punishment can be regarded as adequate recompense for the moral wrong a person has done. Kant has said, after all, that against the ideality of the ethical demand, everyone's guilt is infinite. But if this is so, can anything short of total self-annihilation (moral and spiritual death) make repayment for sin? Dare a person regard the remorse experienced during repentance and any subsequent misfortune as sufficient compensation for his wrong—and if he does so has he not precisely missed the full seriousness of his prior conduct? Paradoxically, the most repentant individual must know how inadequate his repentance is to the demand, while only a shallow conscience can regard repentance as a solution to the problem.

Kant's entire discussion, then, seems to point beyond itself. As a means of moral self-justification, repentance is filled with prob-

---

[37]In the passages that follow these remarks, Kant ingeniously interprets Christ's vicarious atonement as a representation of the essentially vicarious nature of all penitent suffering (ibid., 68f.). This interpretation suggests a further parallel between Kant and Kierkegaard: a shared conviction that the truly Christian life is one characterized by the willing acceptance of suffering.

lems. At the same time, however, it readily gives rise to certain religious ideas that supplement its deficiencies. For example, if the self cannot esteem any suffering it undergoes as adequate repayment for its wrongs, it can hope that this suffering may be regarded as sufficient in the eyes of a more knowledgeable, more objective judge. God plays this role for the religious believer. Similarly, if the self cannot certify its will to be reformed, it can hope that God, who sees the heart and who knows both past and future, will find this changed willing as the beginning of a new personhood. And the self may even hope that its resolve will somehow be assisted by God in the future. Throughout the *Religion* Kant actually explores ideas of this sort. For example, to understand how a change of heart can come about, he says, one may require a notion of divine grace.[38] In some passages, he even perceives a role for active, divine assistance in the process whereby sin is canceled and a new upright will replaces the old.[39] These passages, however, alternate with others that point to the moral difficulties of these ideas—for how, Kant asks, can we be judged morally worthy for what we have not done?[40] Throughout, Kant also insists on the abiding priority of our always first reorienting our will toward the moral law.

As other commentators have noted, in the pages of the *Religion* one sees a great philosopher torn between his own best insights.[41] On one side stands an ethical theory whose premise is man's ability and obligation to perform the moral law. On the other side stands an equally powerful series of ideas spawned by that same ethical theory, including an understanding of the depths of human freedom such that even immoral willing is a rational possibility, a sense of the law's stringent demand before which all stand

---

[38]Ibid., 43, 60, 82.

[39]Ibid., 159, 179.

[40]Ibid., 19, 55, 134, 179.

[41]See, for example, the account of Kant's discussion of grace offered by John R. Silber in his introductory essay, "The Ethical Significance of Kant's *Religion*," in *Religion within the Limits of Reason Alone*, cxxxiiff. For a more sympathetic view see Allen W. Wood, *Kant's Moral Religion* (Ithaca NY: Cornell University Press, 1970) ch. 6.

unjustified, and a corresponding understanding of man's virtual bondage to sin. If the *Religion* repeatedly vacillates between an Enlightenment stress on duty and a more orthodox intimation of the need for grace and faith as a way of completing the moral enterprise, it is because Kant was himself divided on these matters. On the one hand, he was the quintessential Enlightenment philosopher. On the other hand, he was a thinker whose very intellectual power shattered some of the confidences upon which Enlightenment thought was built.

With Kierkegaard one enters another world. His intellectual context, his biography, and his temperament make him fully willing to develop the logic of faith. The difficulties in ethics that, for Kant, were a source of embarrassment, become for Kierkegaard opportunities. Where Kant was perhaps reluctant to develop some of his best insights, Kierkegaard is eager to do so, and Kant's rigorous analysis appears to provide all the occasion he needs.

Everything said here suggests that in Kierkegaard, Kant found one of the best readers of his *Religion within the Limits of Reason Alone.* Not only does Kierkegaard in *The Concept of Anxiety* (and elsewhere in his writings) appear to draw upon key insights presented in the *Religion,* but in some ways, Kierkegaard manages to carry these insights out to the conclusion that Kant, hampered by his own intellectual baggage, was unable to reach.

Did Kierkegaard, then, actually study the *Religion* and draw upon it in writing *The Concept of Anxiety?* This question has been left for last because presently I am unable to answer it. What evidence exists is conflicting and only circumstantial. On one side of the question is the fact that none of the standard biographies mention the extent of Kierkegaard's familiarity with Kant, and Kierkegaard himself nowhere in his papers or writings explicitly mentions the *Religion.*[42] Then, too, there is the fact that at least some of the points explored here—for example, the moral difficulties of repentance—are touched on by thinkers like Fichte and Hegel by

---

[42]Kierkegaard does refer to several of Kant's writings, although he nowhere explicitly refers to the *Religion.* For a listing of these references see JP, 2:611f.; see also Gill, "Kantianism," 228.

whom Kierkegaard was clearly influenced.[43] This connection may suggest a debt to these two nearer figures rather than to Kant. On the other side of the question, there is the fact that Kierkegaard does, at least once, claim familiarity with "Kantian" ethics (EO, 2:327), and he does refer explicitly to Kant's idea of "radical evil," the central concept in the section of the *Religion* explored here (JP, 3:3089). The possibility of a debt to Fichte or Hegel on the points discussed is also somewhat doubtful because both thinkers only mention these issues in passing, and one finds in their work none of the careful analysis that makes Kant's treatment so authoritative.

As is, I must leave this historical and biographical question to others for the time being. What I have tried to do here is at least indicate some major continuities between Kant's *Religion within the Limits of Reason Alone* and Kierkegaard's *Concept of Anxiety*. By pointing these out, I hope to have shed new light on some of the important presuppositions of Kierkegaard's work. I also hope to have indicated a relatively unexplored path—one leading through Kierkegaard—by which Kant's philosophy may have influenced subsequent religious thought.

---

[43]Many of the themes touched upon here resonate within the writings of Fichte and Hegel. For example, Fichte's *Attempt at a Critique of All Revelation*, trans. Garrett Green (Cambridge: Cambridge University Press, 1978) broadly shares Kant's conception of the ideality of morality and is critical of nonmoral or purely "historical" elements in Christian teaching. The section on "Absolute Spirit" in Hegel's *Encyclopedia of Philosophy*, trans. Gustav Emil Mueller (New York: Philosophical Library, 1959) bears some similarities to Kant's discussion of sin and repentance. Hegel's treatment of Adam as a representative type in the *Lectures on the Philosophy of Religion*, trans. E. B. Speirs and J. B. Sanderson (London: Kegan Paul, Trench, Trubner, 1895) especially 1:275-79 and 2:202-204, also displays similarities to the work of Kant and Kierkegaard. But in all of these cases, the resemblances are often faint and the texts are only reminiscent of the more full-bodied Kantian arguments on which they are based.

IV

Schelling and Kierkegaard on Freedom and Fall

by Vincent A. McCarthy

Although Kierkegaard's *The Concept of Anxiety* begins as a reflection upon the first sin, it quickly directs itself to the more profound question of the origins of all sin. Formally, it opens with a discussion of inherited (or original) sin and proceeds to analyze the structure of the human spirit that makes both sin and overcoming sin possible. Central to the structure and the essence of the human spirit are the categories and actualities of freedom and possibility.

Kierkegaard is by no means the only modern thinker to be concerned with sin, possibility, and freedom, or the relation among them. Kant's "On the Radical Evil in Human Nature" (part 1 of *Religion within the Limits of Reason Alone*, 1793) had considered these same subjects and had also philosophically undermined the theological notion of inheriting Adam's first sin. Kant established through a kind of introspective speculation that one's feeling of fallenness and accountability for fall point to a personal deed whose elements can be discerned, even if the when and why of such a deed can never be made clear.

The theodicy question of the eighteenth century was thereby partially answered: man is responsible for moral evil and for his own fall. In 1809 Schelling published a work whose distinctiveness was only much later appreciated, his *Treatise on the Essence of Human Freedom* (hereafter cited as the *Freiheitsschrift*).[1] In publishing his work on freedom, Schelling was emphatically breaking with idealism just as it was completing its transition from subjective idealism (in Fichte) to objective idealism (in Hegel). In it, Schelling too sought to explain moral evil, lay the blame at man's door, and in the process acquit God of any share in it. But Schelling's approach was unique and suggestive in that it acknowledged evil as real and thus as something proceeding from God. Moreover, it did so in such way that God became the ground and source of the possibility of evil without being the creator of evil thereby.

Kierkegaard took up the themes of freedom and fall in his 1844 *Concept of Anxiety*, with his own special emphases. He was interested in a better explanation than the "inherited sin" of dogmatic theology, and he was concerned with observing, via speculative reconstruction, the movements into sin but with the added practical interest of pointing toward the overcoming of sin (something completed in *Sickness Unto Death*, the companion volume to *Concept of Anxiety*).

The foregoing will have suggested the commonsense (but neglected) observation that Kierkegaard takes his ordered place in the history of philosophy and philosophical engagement of individual themes, and that he is therefore less the "exception" than some would have him be. Specifically, Kierkegaard's treatment of freedom and fall is part of a continuum in modern philosophy that in-

---

[1]*Philosophische Untersuchungen über das Wesen der menschlichen Freiheit*, in *Friedrich Wilhelm von Schellings sämtliche Werke*, 14 vols., 2 parts, ed. K. F. A. Schelling (Stuttgart and Augsburg: J. C. Cotta'scher Verlag, 1856-1861), cited as SW 7 hereinafter.

cludes Kant, Fichte, and Schelling. It of course also includes Hegel.[2] On the subject of freedom, the torch passes from Schelling to Kierkegaard (unbeknownst to both), and the treatment of fall is an outgrowth of their respective conceptions of freedom and of their adherence to orthodox Christian interpretation.

Kierkegaard and Schelling

Kierkegaard attended Schelling's Berlin Lectures on the Philosophy of Revelation from November 1841 until about 4 February 1842 when his *Referats*, or lecture notes, break off.[3] Although his letter of 6 February to Emil Boesen says that he will return to Copenhagen when Schelling has finished and that he expects this to be in the spring, his letter of 27 February announces his imminent plans to leave Berlin. An undated letter of the same month to his brother Peter complains that Schelling is taking longer than expected (LD, 141), derides the lecturer for talking "the most insufferable nonsense," and declares his intention to leave Berlin for Copenhagen as soon as possible.

The lecture notes kept by Kierkegaard cease at the point where Schelling is reviewing the relation of his philosophy of mythology to his philosophy of revelation. Kierkegaard thus heard Schelling up to lecture 19 in the published version of the philosophy of revelation.[4] Consequently, Kierkegaard did not hear Schelling's formal treatment of Christianity with its important, if curious, sections of philosophical theogony and "Logogony" in the later lectures, although Kierkegaard had evidently heard enough in preliminary allusions not to be persuaded to remain longer.

---

[2]Some detect the influence of Schleiermacher as well. Cf. the translator's notes to *The Concept of Anxiety*, 228-29, n. 47 and n. 49. A much longer list could be compiled, beginning with Socrates and Aristotle.

[3]Kierkegaard's first journal entry about Schelling's lectures (*Papirer* III A 179; JP, 5355) refers to the second lecture, 11 November 1841. Here too is contained his oft-cited remark about the babe in his womb who leapt for joy upon hearing a philosopher speak at last of "actuality."

[4]*Philosophie der Offenbarung;* SW 13-14.

Why rehearse such details? The reason is simple: of all the German thinkers that Kierkegaard learned from and reacted to, Schelling is the only one that Kierkegaard actually heard and saw. Kierkegaard's 1841 sojourn in Berlin, after his break with Regine Olsen, is a well-known episode from his biography-laden writings. His early hopes and enthusiasm about Schelling, and his almost immediate disappointment, are almost equally well known.

However, the full story of Kierkegaard's encounter with Schelling's philosophy has not been told. Indeed, it has hardly begun to be told, and in great part because of a preoccupation with Hegel in Kierkegaard studies.[5] Nor can this essay pretend to remedy the neglect. At best, it will be a modest beginning. Indeed, the themes of *The Concept of Anxiety* suggest comparison with Schelling. But there is an additional reason that singles out this particular Kierkegaard work for beginning a Kierkegaard-Schelling comparison: Of the eleven references to Schelling cited in the McKinnon indices to Kierkegaard's *Samlede Vaerke*, nine of them occur in *Concept of Anxiety*.[6]

Despite Kierkegaard's 1842 dismissal of Professor Schelling, there are resonances and striking similarities with Schelling's ideas (as well as differences) in his subsequent works. A draft introduction to *Repetition* in 1843[7] refers several times to Schelling's 1809 essay on human freedom.[8] It is not possible to determine from these

---

[5]But even Kant is neglected in Kierkegaard studies, although a fine essay on this very subject is contained in this IKC volume. One frequently feels that Kierkegaard is reacting to Kantian material, particularly to *Religion within the Limits of Reason Alone*, and this would have been expected in religious philosophy of the German-speaking world even into the middle of the nineteenth century. The sense of unannounced dialogue with Kant is especially strong in *Fear and Trembling*. Cf. Robert L. Perkins, "For Sanity's Sake: Kant, Kierkegaard and Father Abraham" in his *Kierkegaard's* Fear and Trembling: *Critical Appraisals* (University AL: University of Alabama Press, 1981) 43-61.

[6]There is a single reference to "Schelling" in *Concluding Unscientific Postscript* and another to "Schellings" in *Either/Or*. In addition, there is a single mention of "Schellings" in *The Concept of Irony*. There are also four adjectival references ("schellingske"), but *The Concept of Anxiety*'s being the preeminent locus of Schelling discussion is not undercut thereby.

[7]*Papirer* IV B 117 and 118.

[8]*Schelling: Of Human Freedom*, trans. James Gutmann (Chicago: Open Court Publishing House, 1936), hereinafter cited as the *Freiheitsschrift*.

references when precisely Kierkegaard read the essay, whether before or after his encounter with Schelling in Berlin. Based on the 1843 publication date of two works by Rosenkranz on Schelling, works that Kierkegaard read and referred to in writings of this period (*Sendschreiben an P. Leroux über Schelling und Hegel* and *Vorlesungen über Schelling*), I believe that Kierkegaard's emphasis on Schelling in his drafts and publications of 1843-1844 suggests a careful reading of the *Freiheitsschrift* in 1843, or at least a rereading prompted by Rosenkranz's works.[9] In addition, it would be most unlikely that this important Schelling work, which had not received much comment at the time of its publication, would have come so early to the attention of a faraway Dane—hence, an even stronger reason for leaning toward the theory of a later reading.

Most important about the *Freiheitsschrift* for my purposes here is that the notion of good and evil presented in it suggests rich comparison with Kierkegaard's discussion in *Concept of Anxiety*. Had Kierkegaard kept notes on this work, they would have been enormously valuable in assessing Kierkegaard in relation to the critique of idealism, since the *Freiheitsschrift* was the intellectual abdication and attempted slaying of idealism by one of its founding figures. In it, as Heidegger has noted, Schelling saw through the problems of idealist metaphysics before Hegel's *Logic* was set to paper.[10] Kierkegaard does not seem to have perceived Schelling's accomplishment, nor is Schelling invoked in Kierkegaard's criticism of Hegel.[11]

Schelling considered his philosophy of revelation to be a "positive philosophy" and a philosophy of freedom. It was to be "positive" in contrast to the "negative" that, in Schelling's view, had

---

[9]Cf. n. 17 to chapter 1 of *The Concept of Anxiety*.

[10]*Schellings Abhandlung über das Wesen der Menschlichen Freiheit*, ed. Hildegard Feich (Tübingen: Niemayer Verlag, 1971) 117. Heidegger provides a rich commentary on Schelling's work. His *Being and Time* also amply elaborates on Kierkegaard's notion of anxiety, although Heidegger does not give proper credit to Kierkegaard on this and other points.

[11]All of which may only serve to underline the view that Kierkegaard's polemic was more essentially and substantially directed against Copenhagen Hegelians than against Hegel himself.

culminated in Hegel. Its very fundament was to be freedom—and this in conscious antithesis to the category necessity in the Hegelian system. On the basis of this fundament, a fully detailed philosophy of freedom was to be constructed, of which the philosophy of revelation would be the culminating section. The philosophy of revelation is, however, the only section that is complete, and it is not a polished piece. A full positive philosophy or philosophy of freedom would require a philosophy of existence, which Schelling did not supply. (Heidegger comments that this ambition is tantamount to a squared circle,[12] and Kierkegaard, without any reference to Schelling on this point, declares that a system of existence is impossible [CUP, 107] precisely because of freedom.)

The application of the philosophy of freedom in the philosophy of revelation is indeed curious at times, but it bears reviewing precisely because Kierkegaard listened to it in 1841 and then wrote about some of the same themes in 1843 and 1844. The philosophy of freedom expressed in 1841 develops the earlier effort in the unpublished Munich lectures of 1831 and is an outgrowth of the more important *Freiheitsschrift*. But the discussion of Schelling's works here will follow the order in which I believe Kierkegaard came to know them. Hence, I proceed from the 1841 lectures on the philosophy of revelation to the 1809 *Freiheitsschrift*, and then to Kierkegaard's 1844 *The Concept of Anxiety*.

Freedom and Fall
in the Philosophy of Revelation

Schelling's God-concept lies at the center of the philosophy of revelation. In a sense, his God-concept is the philosophy of revelation, for all its major themes in effect elaborate on God's life. Schelling stresses God in process, a living God who realizes and manifests himself in freely creating and redeeming a world. Moreover, in actualizing himself, he attains a personhood that was only potential prior to creation. Schelling wished at every point to avoid any suggestion of necessity in creation or in God's life (and spe-

---

[12]*Schellings Abhandlung*, 26.

cifically anything resembling emanationism). He also wished to ward off any appearance of pantheism, while at the same time validating pantheism and polytheism as important phases in the history of religion that were part of the restoration of monotheism. In addition, since the creation is free and unnecessary, it is in no way required of God that he become incarnate and person. Thus, when he becomes a person, he does so freely.[13]

The details of God's life are set forth in the darkest teaching of the philosophy of revelation, Schelling's doctrine of potencies. Potency is at the center of all that is living, according to Schelling, including the living God. Schelling's is by no means a satisfying or even persuasive teaching, but it remains a central one and is of interest for its parallel to that which underlies the dizziness of freedom in Kierkegaard's *The Concept of Anxiety*. Schelling set forth his obscure theory in lectures 10-14. Kierkegaard bore up under it, although he snapped that the doctrine of potencies betrayed the greatest impotence (LD, 141).

The doctrine is tied to the root teaching of God's freedom and attempts to explain how *all* freedom—including divine freedom—moves from the nothingness of possibility into actuality. In it, Schelling steers equally away from creation ex nihilo and from emanationism. The latter is avoided because it is a product of necessity. Schelling avoids the former since he will have God create not out of pure nothingness but rather out of that-which-is-not-yet, not out of οὐκ ὄν but out of μὴ ὄν. Schelling's distinction revolves around a subtle difference in Greek negatives. In οὐκ ὄν the emphasis is on the negative (οὐκ) and the term signifies that which *is not* and *cannot be*. In μὴ ὄν the emphasis is on being (ὄν) and the term thus signifies that which is *not presently actual*. Whatever is μὴ ὄν, while not presently actual, *can be*. And it is out of this "can be," or potency, which Schelling conceives of as part of God and yet apart from God, that creation—and all that happens in and to creation—is held to arise.

---

[13]Schelling's heavy emphasis on freedom is not without its price. For, since the incarnation of God is not necessary, it is in a sense unessential, and with this arises connotations of ultimately being not just "accidental" but "incidental" as well.

The first potency, which is Able-To-Be (A^1), is also that which Ought-Not-To-Be. Yet in fact this potency has been actualized: that which is able-to-be and ought-not-to-be has come to be. Having done so, it must go further, on to resolution, by moving *ab actu ad potentiam:* by progressing from actualization to restoration as pure potency. This resolution is caused by the movement of the second potency that, in fulfilling itself, restores the original potency of A^1. Schelling's obscure mathematical notations A^1, A^2, and A^3 take on new meaning when one learns that A^1 refers to the Fall, A^2 to God's Logos who restores, and A^3 to the Spirit. The full actualization of the potencies thus represents fall and restoration but also—and synonymously—the actualized life of God, or theogony. Ultimately, the three potencies come to stand for the trinitarian life of God and the three personalities of God's life that result from the process. (For the Logos [A^2] is held to have been divine but not fully God before actualization and at the end to enter into Godhead—a point expanded upon in the Christology section that Kierkegaard never heard.)

All three potencies are potencies of God's being. God is thus the source of all being and of all potency. He is the lord of possibilities, actualized and/or unactualized. Moreover, he would be fully and really God even as lord of mere potencies, had he never actualized a world.[14] This point contrasts with negative philosophy's (that is, Hegel's) suggestion that God would not be God without a world, by which creation is reduced to a divine necessity and is hence unfree.

As the Logos or second potency (A^2) actualizes itself, creation is restored. And he, along with the actualized Spirit, comes then to constitute God as a trinity of actualized persons. This constitutes theogony, or God's becoming. All three members of the potentially actual Trinity were active in creation. All three in fact acted as creator: the creator as Father is he who goes out in exclusive being, the creator as Son is he who overcomes this exclusive being, and the creator as Spirit is he who completes or perfects arisen being. In this, the Father provides the "stuff" of creation and is its

---

[14]Lecture 14; SW 13:291.

material cause; the Son gives creaturely form and is thus its formal cause; while the Spirit as the common will of both brings creation to what it should be, perfects it, and is thus its final cause.[15]

The second part of Schelling's lectures outlines the place of man in creation and the role he plays in God's theogony.[16] Creation has not followed its ideal course—not because of any necessity but because of freedom. In this instance it is the freedom of the human creature that does the deed. Man had been made the lord of causes (*Ursachen*), but only insofar as he preserved their unity. However, he wished to be lord of potencies or like God. Mankind, who would be lord of potencies in their dispersal and not just in their unity, set the potencies in opposition. In doing this, he made himself lord of the world, but lord of a fallen world "outside God." Alienation of the world from God is thus man's free deed. Schelling's philosophical account of the Fall is, admittedly, replete with problems. Moreover, like many such accounts—and like the accounts of both Kant and Kierkegaard—in the end it only indicates that something occurred and not why.

In sum, man, by setting the potencies in opposition, is responsible for the entrance of evil into the world. The alienation or extradivinity of the world vis-à-vis God is thus not the result of any cause independent of God, even if it proceeds originally from God. Man's desire or will to be like God led him demonically to wreak havoc upon the created world. In the process, he succeeded in becoming "like God," but not God-like, for the usurper emerged as the perverse lord of being. A striking variation from other accounts of the Fall is Schelling's having the Son or Logos immediately and freely follow creation into alienation or extradivinity, in order to restore it from within at a later point.[17]

---

[15]Schelling finds this reading of Aristotle into the Trinity supported by St. Paul himself in the Epistle to the Romans (11:36) where the apostle speaks of all that is created as "from him, through him and in him." The principal novelty of this reading consists in the view of the Son as formal cause or demiurge.

[16]In Kierkegaard potency, or potentiality, plays a role in what might be called "anthropogony," or humankind's becoming process, and as such is really a parallel notion, only reduced to the human plane.

[17]This might sound Manichaean, except that in the Manichaean teaching primal man is taken prisoner in the creation and is thus under a kind of necessity.

God's free creation has now broken with him, and he maintains it in existence for the sake of eventual restoration by the Son/ Logos. This will be a great good for the world, but also for God, who becomes actualized as Trinity in the process. Both creation and redemption are free, and both are part of God's life or theogony. Freedom and Fall are thus accounted for, as well as the outlines of redemption. (While Schelling's God is free, he would seem to be the unfortunate victim of caprice in his own creation. He allows free actions that affect not only creation but also his own being. And he might even appear foolish to some for having allowed himself to be determined by others' use and misuse of God-given freedom.)

Kierkegaard heard this much and heard also the details of the time of the suffering of the Son of Man. Schelling describes the Son of Man as the hidden principle of paganism present while paganism struggled—under necessity—toward restored monotheism, when the Son freely revealed himself in Christianity. Kierkegaard's *Referat* breaks off during the survey of the pagan mysteries, just after the discussion of Demeter and Persephone, still well before the large-scale Christology and philosophical interpretation of the Christian religion. Kierkegaard had obviously heard enough, realized his hopes for a significant new philosophy from Schelling were to be disappointed, and left Berlin.[18] Yet the attentive listener who is familiar with Kierkegaard's own writings will have heard echoes already of positions Kierkegaard himself was to take in *Concept of Anxiety*. But before he did so, he read, or at least reread, Schelling's earlier work of 1809, in which Shelling first discussed potency, freedom, and Fall.

Freedom and Fall
in Of Human Freedom

Schelling's philosophy of revelation is a philosophy of religion that tries to build upon the conviction that man is a *free* being in a *free* universe that has been created by and is ruled over by a *free*,

---

[18]He departed the Prussian capital on 6 March 1842, approximately one month after his *Referat* breaks off. Whether he attended additional lectures without note-taking is unclear, but it is unlikely that he did.

personal, and living God with whom he is in relation, not just in thought but in experience, and most centrally through the experience of God's *free* revelation.

But the emphasis on freedom began much earlier. Schelling had come to see that things were not as they ought to be. (Biography may have played some role here, for the untimely death of Caroline Schlegel Schelling occurred during this period.) In short, the world of actuality was not the world that thought would have had him expect, following through the necessary stages that thought discerns. As he was driven to ask why actuality does not correspond to thought, he was quickly carried beyond his original philosophy of identity and its point of departure in the identity of thought and being. In this, he radically confronted the issue of human freedom, something that idealism, in his view, had not solved but merely subsumed into necessity. While Schelling did not revert to Kant's noumenal/phenomenal distinction to overcome this philosophical/existential antinomy, he was, like Kant, gradually pressed to philosophically engage the reality of evil. In doing so, Schelling pursued freedom back to God himself and, out of the hazy sequence Eternal God-Creation-Fall, derived a new doctrine of creation according to which creation did not issue from pure nothingness (οὐκ ὄν) but from nonbeing (μὴ ὄν). This was the theory that was elaborated in the doctrine of potencies and the view of theogony both in 1809 and 1841.

In its fundamental thesis of human freedom grounded in a divine freedom, the *Freiheitsschrift* made its self-conscious break with idealism. Freedom, for Schelling, was defined as in effect a nonsensuous feeling[19] and, as Heidegger put it, "the original feeling for the unity of all being in and out of its ground."[20]

In order to preserve his fledgling concept of freedom from being reabsorbed by idealism, Schelling had emphatically refused to view freedom as standing in a dialectical relationship to an antithetical concept of necessity. Thus, freedom for Schelling consists of ne-

---

[19]Heidegger, *Schellings Abhandlung*, 18.

[20]Ibid., 82-83.

cessity, and necessity consists of freedom.[21] And the separation
between freedom and necessity remained the most fundamental
category distinction for him. In his view, it was more important
than the separation between essence and existence that leads to
philosophical errors (by which he meant those of Hegel), since it
is not fundamental enough. It is also more fundamental than the
separation between possibility and actuality.

For Schelling then, only a philosophy that built upon the deepest fundament and that recognized the relationship between the
fundamental categories (in this instance, a nondialectical relationship) could issue in a correct philosophical system. His point was
two-sided: the Hegelian model that was dialectical, based on the
logical relationship between being and nonbeing, was not fundamental enough; the new model, his own, was built instead on a
fundamental, nondialectical relationship as manifested not in any
idea but in the phenomenon of freedom. The consequence of this
position was far-reaching: a revision of the entire enterprise of philosophy was necessary in light of the newly attained perspective
of freedom. But if Schelling was freed from certain idealist presuppositions, he was still not freed from the idealist ambition of system construction. He still held to a "system of freedom" as his goal.
But to construct such a system of freedom, a mode of knowledge
had to be sought that went beyond mere ideas and logical necessity. Schelling sought a historical philosophy of actualized freedom, and this ultimately issued in the philosophy of freedom and,
more specifically, the philosophy of revelation, in which the revelation of the Christian religion is taken as the record of actualized
freedom and the key to interpreting all that had gone before.[22]

The new philosophy demanded by the fact of human freedom
had to account for the ground of this freedom, and specifically for
the God that was its ultimate source. Hence, it was required to account for divine freedom too. This meant recasting the conception
of God, and Schelling's philosophy of revelation finally had to rec-

---

[21]Cf. Walter Kasper, *Das Absolute in der Geschichte* (Mainz: Matthias-Grüne-
wald Verlag, 1965) 212.

[22]Even if it is a key that only Schelling's own philosophy can turn.

oncile what he viewed as God's essentially in-itself *completed* being with the freedom that God exercises.[23]

The God-concept of the *Freiheitsschrift* describes two equally eternal beginnings in God, a God with two poles: (1) God as conscious subject and (2) the dark ground of God, which is not conscious, which is inseparable from God and yet also different. This dark ground is not only the ground for the becoming of all that is not God (in particular, the world) but also for the becoming of God himself. With this, Schelling sought to describe a living God who is his own creator and who is ground and creator of both that which will be apart from him and that which he himself will become. But the condition for the possibility of a becoming, or existing God, is at the same time the condition for the possibility of good and evil.[24]

The bipolar God-concept revolutionized Schelling's philosophical standpoint in 1809 and also contained within it an explanation of freedom (both divine and human), an explanation of the Fall, and the seeds of a theodicy. For evil could now be understood as real, as proceeding from the dark ground of God, and thus grounded, like all that is real, in God himself. The notion situated all within God's being, yet allowed for differences and contradiction—even to the extent of evil—without thereby compromising the notion of God as good or being obliged to embrace a good/evil dualism. How could a good God permit evil? The age-old question of theodicy found a new explanation: All that is and that has come to be proceeds from the dark ground of God, including that which ought not to be. Why is there not perfection from the beginning? Simply put: because God is a life.[25]

The *Freiheitsschrift* of 1809 set out to account for human freedom in ways that thought would not expect, explained evil and the Fall on the basis of human freedom, then sought to go further in order to explain the metaphysical relationship of human freedom to God and to God's own freedom.

---

[23]Cf. Horst Fuhrmans, *Schellings letzte Philosophie* (Berlin, 1940) 64.

[24]Cf. Heidegger, *Schellings Abhandlung*, 143.

[25]*Freiheitsschrift* (SW 7), 403; English trans., 84.

In sum, freedom has its base in the dark ground of God, a darkness that is the source of all potential and hence the source of potential good as well as potential evil. The possibility of good and evil is thus contained in God himself, even while God remains all good. For God creates only what is good. But within his creation is a creature by nature good but endowed with freedom and hence with the potential to choose to actualize good and/or evil. Historically, this creature chose to actualize evil and thereby perverted the original order of creation: the aboriginal unity of creation was shattered and evil; that which ought-not-to-be was actualized.[26]

Certain emphases immediately emerge. First, man himself is responsible for evil. No evil spirit tempts him in Schelling's account; the blame cannot be shifted or shared. God created a good world that man perverted. God is thereby absolved from responsibility for evil even while the possibility of evil is located in the dark ground of God's own being.

But while Schelling sought to avoid all dualisms of either a Zoroastrian or Manichaean kind, God seems to have become dualistic in any case. He is not, to be sure, a God of good and evil. But he is a God of light and darkness—the latter being his dark ground that contains all potentiality. And evil arises from this dark ground, although only through the mediation of other actualities, namely, the world and mankind. The world and mankind, themselves products of the dark ground of God, have potential, or their own dark ground, and, alas, actualize evil. (It was, of course, not necessary that evil be actualized.)

Evil is thus real, as are the good, creation, and man. They are all the product of the freedom that is able to act on the potential for good and evil. God, who is free and who has such potential, acts and creates the good. But one good that he creates has its own potential, and in the exercise of its freedom, brings forth evil. Schelling's treatise *Of Human Freedom* thus begins with the theme

---

[26]Despite his new theodicy, Schelling would not really escape his French Enlightenment predecessors' rebukes regarding philosophical attempts to justify God. One might well imagine a Voltaire's reaction to the account of a God who does not need a world but then creates one anyway, and, alas, such a troublesome and manifestly mixed world at that. A *philosophe* might well have quipped that perhaps if God had needed the world, he might have created a better one!

proclaimed in its title but quickly moves on, stimulated by the misuse of human freedom to probe the very structure of divine freedom.

Freedom and Fall
in The Concept of Anxiety

Kierkegaard does not begin where Schelling ended, nor begin where Schelling begins. Nor does he retrace Schelling's steps. His enterprise is different. He begins with a different problem and a different method. The movement from Schelling to Kierkegaard is thus somewhat of a leap, and yet the ground covered is not so different. Kierkegaard's slim volume (published under the pseudonym Vigilius Haufniensis) begins with sin, and with the particular dogmatic issue of hereditary sin. Yet in analyzing it, Kierkegaard traces much the same intellectual terrain as Schelling, albeit in a different sequence. Kierkegaard begins with the first sin rather than with what made it possible, emphasizes this first sin (known as hereditary or original sin) as belonging to the genus rather than being *sui generis*, and then penetrates to the deeper ground of sin in freedom. In pursuing a Kierkegaard-Schelling comparison, discussion is confined to the relevant sections of *The Concept of Anxiety*, that is, to chapters 1 and 2.

What most immediately distinguishes Kierkegaard's treatment from Schelling's is that Kierkegaard does not carry the analysis of human freedom back to God and divine freedom. But the workings of human freedom are essentially the same for both. How human freedom relates structurally to God's being is simply not a theme of Kierkegaard's work. And yet it cannot be radically different from Schelling's conception either, even if Kierkegaard would never seriously entertain the details of Schelling's theogony.[27]

The Concept of Anxiety begins with the dogmatic problem of inherited or original sin in chapter 1 but quickly uses this as a spring-

---

[27]Kierkegaard's thin pseudonym Vigilius Haufniensis is really theologically quite orthodox, notwithstanding his argument over the proper interpretation of hereditary sin.

board for a discussion of sin in general and of the more practical matter of overcoming sin. For, once it is established that each brings sin into the world for himself, the important practical question emerges concerning the exercise of freedom and actualization of human possibility in overcoming sin—subjects that extend beyond the scope of Haufniensis's work but lie within the scope of Anti-Climacus's in *The Sickness Unto Death*.

"[N]o explanation," writes Haufniensis, "that explains Adam but not hereditary sin, or explains hereditary sin but not Adam, is of any help" (CA, 28). Ultimately, Kierkegaard-Haufniensis seeks an explanation that will explain Everyman and every sin. Kierkegaard's interest in the Fall is thus universal, whereas Schelling's is particular. The interest of each in freedom is universal, while Schelling's is the more complete since he includes God. However, while Schelling's discussion of the Fall confines itself to Adam's, there is no inherent reason why it could not be applied to other humans, and indeed such application is implicit. For Schelling would recognize all as fallen and all as having exercised the same freedom that Adam had.

The first sin emerges not from a state of sinfulness but from innocence, and Haufniensis-Kierkegaard's consideration turns to a psychological (but hardly empirical) investigation of spirit in its original dreaming and innocence.

> In innocence . . . there is peace and repose, but there is simultaneously something else that is not contention and strife, for there is indeed nothing against which to strive. What, then, is it? Nothing. But what effect does nothing have? It begets anxiety. (CA, 41)

"Nothing" acts as "something." Moreover, it is not outside but within: "Dreamily the spirit projects its own actuality, but this actuality is nothing, and innocence always sees this nothing outside" (CA, 41). "Nothing" begets freedom's reality as the possibility for possibility. The anxiety spoken of is the anxiety that emerges in innocence. This is not the whole of anxiety, but only its beginning.

The passage goes on to observe that anxiety has the same significance for dreaming spirit that melancholy or "heavy-spiritedness" (*Tungsind*) has at a later point (CA, 42). Not only does

Kierkegaard see the connection between anxiety and melancholy, but also Schelling saw the very same connection of conditions (he never used the term *anxiety*). In the *Freiheitsschrift*, he spoke of the dark ground of God as a condition relatively independent of him. This is God's unactualized potential, or one might say that "God's Nothing" is a source of melancholy or "heavy-spiritedness" to him, and more—to the whole creation in which this nothing or dark ground is found.[28] "Thus the veil of sadness (*Schwermuth*) which is spread over all nature, the deep, unappeasable melancholy (*Melancholie*) of all life." The English translations of both Kierkegaard and Schelling are misleading here, for the connection is stronger still. Both German and Danish have two terms for melancholy, and Schelling and Kierkegaard employ both.[29] Danish *Tungsind* and German *Schwermuth* are the normal translations for each other. They both translate literally as *heavy-spiritedness* and represent a graver form of melancholy. Hence, the spiritual problem of *Tungsind* that Kierkegaard alludes to is really quite allied to the *Schwermuth* that Schelling speaks of in God and in all nature. *Tungsind* and *Schwermuth* are products of the nothingness contained in every and all being and lead to the actualization of freedom's possibilities.[30]

The Genesis prohibition induces anxiety and desire in Adam, and this awakens spirit that was innocent and ignorant (CA, 44). Spirit seeks knowledge by use of its freedom. Anxiety is the product of an unqualified "being able," of the nothing—or "dark ground"—of the spirit. Kierkegaard does not make the connection, but his "nothing" and Schelling's "dark ground" are parallel categories and function very similarly. They are the unactualized potential that is part of every individual and that rises up to confront him.

---

[28]SW 7; English trans., 79.

[29]The passage from Schelling's *Freiheitsschrift* with the two German words also happens to be one of the two passages of this work that Kierkegaard refers to in *The Concept of Anxiety*. He does not, however, comment on the distinction to which I have referred.

[30]For a fuller discussion of *Melancholi* and *Tungsind* in Kierkegaard—and the differences between them—cf. Vincent A. McCarthy, "Melancholy and Religious Melancholy in Kierkegaard," *Kierkegaardiana* 10, 151-65. Also, *The Phenomenology of Moods in Kierkegaard* (The Hague and Boston: Martinus Nijhoff, 1978) 53-81.

Anxiety is the presupposition of hereditary sin (CA, 46) and no anterior condition of sinfulness serves in its stead. The notion of sinfulness as presupposition for sin is, he holds, an absurd view in the case of Adam, since sinfulness entered the world for the first time in Adam's deed. But Kierkegaard stresses that such a view is equally mistaken if applied to Adam's descendents. He demands a universally valid explanation without exceptions. Having explained the psychological and metaphysical conditions in which the first sin took place (and in which every first sin and fall must occur), Kierkegaard turns in chapter 2 to the consequences of this deed. For any possibility that has been actualized affects future possibilities. To use Schelling's terminology, that which was able-to-be but that ought-not-to-have-been has come to be. Both ignorance and innocence are past, and present possibilities are modified by the actualized possibility of sin.

Anxiety has now come to mean two things:

> the anxiety in which the individual posits sin by the qualitative leap, and the anxiety that entered in and enters in with sin, and also that, accordingly, enters qualitatively into the world every time an individual posits sin. (CA, 54)

The discussion then turns briefly to objective anxiety before rejoining Kierkegaard's preeminent interest: subjective anxiety.[31]

The anxiety now to be considered is anxiety after the first sin; it is subjective. Of course, strictly speaking, Adam's sin was also the result of subjective anxiety. In this section, the link between anxiety, freedom, and sin becomes clearest.

> Anxiety may be compared with dizziness. He whose eye happens to look down into the yawning abyss becomes dizzy. But what is the reason for this? It is just as much in his own eye as in the abyss, for suppose he had not looked down. Hence anxiety is the dizziness of freedom, which emerges when the spirit wants to posit the synthesis and freedom looks down into its own possibility, laying hold of finiteness to support itself. Freedom succumbs in this diz-

---

[31]Objective anxiety is considered all too briefly. Kierkegaard really does not accord this important category its due and neglects the additional reflection that is warranted regarding the effects of incremental sinfulness in and upon the creation.

ziness. Further than this, psychology cannot and will not go. In that very moment, everything is changed, and freedom, when it again rises, sees that it is guilty. Between these two moments lies the leap, which no science has explained and which no science can explain. (CA, 61)

Freedom succumbs in the dizziness, but the subject is responsible for his own fall.

Such subjective anxiety describes the condition from which every individual arises to discover that he has fallen into sin. Freedom is of course not thereby extinguished, nor is anxiety gone. Possibility remains, an especially important one. From the subject's first sin arise many possibilities but one decisive alternative: either remaining in sin or overcoming it. This either/or is the problem that much of Kierkegaard's aesthetic writings revolve around. Kierkegaard's own interest in overcoming sin is the concern of chapter 5 ("Anxiety as Saving through Faith") and then continued in Anti-Climacus's companion work, *Sickness Unto Death.*

For Kierkegaard then, sin and the overcoming of sin[32] are possibilities fraught with the anxiety produced by the nothingness that is human possibility. Kierkegaard is describing here the ontological structure of the human person as comprised of being and nonbeing. Freedom qualifies the person and acts upon the nonbeing or unactualized potential that is a part of human being.[33]

Spirit is at first nothing more than a possibility that must be awakened and actualized by using its freedom and actualizing its possibility. But its first choice—symbolically expressed in the violation of the divine prohibition in the Garden—is a choice of self against God rather than a choice of self in relation (of obedience) to God. Adam and Everyman were free to do this, and did so. But the action can be overcome, and the miracle of the *felix culpa* is that a greater good will be brought out of this actualized possibility: the Incarnation of God's Son and the Atonement. (On this point, Kier-

---

[32]The latter being the only subject of practical interest since *all* have already fallen, individually.

[33]The suggested dialectic of being and nonbeing evokes Hegel, of course, particularly his *Logic.* The difference here is between a free and existential dialectic rather than a necessary and logical one.

kegaard is orthodox, whereas Schelling turns speculative and fanciful.)

After the first exercise of freedom, freedom and freedom's possibilities remain, with the one important exception of the possibility of sinlessness and innocence that has been annulled. The nothing of anxiety will appear again, and the dialectic of "something" (the actualized self) and "nothing" (possible self) will continue as long as there is life.

For Schelling, the dark ground, too, was there at the beginning—even at the very beginning with God himself—and was there at the moment of the Fall and thereafter. It is the source of the exercise of freedom, for freedom acts upon possibility and makes "something" out of what was "nothing." The ground of freedom is God, and this idea is implicit in Kierkegaard's thought. Hence, Schelling and Kierkegaard share the same metaphysical backdrop of human freedom, namely, divine freedom. And freedom acts upon the potential called by Schelling the "dark ground" and by Kierkegaard the "nothing" that is something. Out of potential have come good and evil, as both Schelling and Kierkegaard observe. The actualization of evil should not have come about, but did so by the misuse of human freedom. And both agree that mankind is responsible for Fall.

At this point, Schelling and Kierkegaard diverge, mostly because the very structure of their respective works takes the discussion in different directions. Schelling really stops with Adam's misuse of freedom and pursues freedom back into the life of God. Kierkegaard is concerned with the freedom and anxiety problem of subjects after Adam and so continues on into greater detail and finer distinctions in the concept of anxiety. Schelling's interest is more metaphysical and theological, whereas Kierkegaard's is psychological and anthropological, but this division is a loose one. Each crosses over, explicitly and implicitly.

Kierkegaard's work gives a new name to Schelling's dark ground, namely, "nothing," and, more important, names its first product: anxiety. Kierkegaard goes on to describe the dynamic of man's dark ground in detail that far surpasses Schelling's work or its ambition. In addition, and an important distinction between the two, Kierkegaard always confines his analysis of freedom to the human plane. God's own dark ground, or nothing, is a subject never broached by Kierkegaard.

It has been clear to many that the existentialist writings of Heidegger and Sartre (and others) are indebted to Kierkegaard for the theme of anxiety, and to both Schelling and Kierkegaard for the issue of freedom as the decisive divide from idealism. But Schelling and Kierkegaard are not so entirely different as Kierkegaard's rejection of Professor Schelling in 1842 might lead one to believe. Kierkegaard's "nothing" indeed seems only another name for the dark ground that underlies the freedom concept in Schelling's work. If there is not conscious influence, there is very probably an unconscious influence of the elder anti-Hegelian upon the younger. There is also an element of continuity between Schelling and Kierkegaard that Kierkegaard himself never seems to realize. Moreover, there is significant parallelism between their respective works with regard to human freedom.

This is not to suggest that Kierkegaard belongs to a Schelling school. Their differences are striking and fundamental: Schelling is a philosopher trying to harmonize his cultural Christianity with his own intellectual experiments; Kierkegaard is an orthodox Christian writer interested in highlighting the distinctiveness of what he held to be Christian truths so that people might in their own interests act upon them and not merely think about them. Freedom and Fall are thus very different themes for both authors, however much the similar dynamic views of freedom lead to novel reinterpretations of the traditional Christian teaching of the Fall.

Kierkegaard "fails" one of his own purposes, of course. He has left much to be thought about, rather than just acted upon. Prominent in this regard is the relationship of his own thought and insights to those of his predecessors and contemporaries. And, where Schelling is concerned, much more remains to be explored.

V

Of Time and Eternity

by Louis Dupré

Schelling's Impact

In *The Concept of Anxiety*, Kierkegaard first sketched the principles of a religious anthropology, which he developed more systematically in *The Sickness Unto Death*, his other "psychological" study. The earlier work remains important for several reasons. It introduces a new method of theological reflection and provides one of the principal categories through which our own epoch has come to understand itself. But its most significant contribution, doubtlessly, lies in a theory of the self as a self-realizing yet dependent synthesis. In the following essay I shall analyze the crucial element

of this anthropological synthesis: the relation between the eternal
and the temporal.

> Man, then, is a synthesis of psyche and body, but he is also a *syn-*
> *thesis of the temporal and the eternal.* That this has often been stated,
> I do not object at all, for it is not my wish to discover something
> new, but rather it is my joy and dearest occupation to ponder out
> that which is quite simple. (CA, 85)

The somewhat polemical tone of this passage as well as the
comparison with earlier theories, the denseness of the text itself,
here and in the corresponding description in *The Sickness Unto*
Death, strongly suggest the impact of other theories. Kierkegaard
felt, of course, no compunction about borrowing from others, nor
did he attempt to hide his sources. In *The Concept of Anxiety* overt
references abound. Yet none support his central definition of the
self. This absence should alert one to the probability of interpre-
tative problems. If Kierkegaard fails to name his predecessors while
generally admitting their existence, his reason for doing so must
be either that he has fundamentally transformed the original theories or that he has so thoroughly assimilated what he has borrowed that he considers it his own. In either case the text invites a
critical comparison with earlier theories.

Undoubtedly, Kierkegaard's principal source for his dynamic
theory of the self is Schelling's *Philosophical Investigations on the Es-*
sence of Human Freedom (1809). In this work, interesting in its own
right (Heidegger devoted a series of lectures to it in 1936), Schelling reformulated the problem of freedom in a manner that has remained influential to the present day. From Descartes to Kant the
question of physical determinism dominated the discussion of
freedom. In Schelling's panentheistic perspective, its integration
with an absolute totality became the critical issue. How can a free
agent remain autonomous while being part of a wider absolute?
Kant had skirted the problem when he considered (and dismissed)
the possibility of a moral theonomy. His primary concern had remained with the possibility of free actions in a physically determined universe. For Schelling the more important question was the
relation of freedom to a transcendent absolute. In modern terms:
How can the preexistence of *given ideals* fail to jeopardize moral au-

tonomy? Authentic freedom tolerates no predetermined order of values or ideals. In his answer Schelling also anticipates modern solutions. God does not predetermine freedom, but, rather, is the very source of man's self-determining activity. Hence, a dependence on the absolute lies at the very roots of moral autonomy. To render this solution acceptable, Schelling first had to neutralize the fear of pantheism that had led to the unbridgeable chasm between the Absolute and the finite free agent. The agent does not relate to God as he relates to the physical world. His activity must at some point *coincide* with a divine creativity on which it intrinsically depends. Man is most intimately united with God when he is free. Opposition begins where freedom ends.

But how can such a God-like freedom include a capacity for evil? To solve this formidable problem, Schelling distinguishes the ground of God's existence from that existence itself. This "Nature-in-God," as he calls it, remains, of course, inseparable from God's Being, yet since it does not coincide with that Being, it *is* not God, but rather the ground from which God himself, as well as all creation, emerges. Man, as the only creature to rise from this dark ground to the full clarity of a spiritual existence, displays a unique resemblance to God, a resemblance that in fact rests upon a partial identity. Only in him is the Word fully spoken and does spirit become manifest. Still, while attaining individual form in the clarity of spirit, man also remains attached to the indeterminate Ground from which he emerges. In God nature and spirit are indissolubly united. In man their bond remains fragile, ever to be strengthened anew. Endowed with spirit, he *is* not simply spirit. At any time he may disturb the delicate balance between spiritual selfhood and dark Nature. Neglecting one or the other, he separates his particular will from the divine will. Schelling's interpretation of moral evil is at once dualistic (in God) and qualifiedly monistic (in man).

In his discussion of original sin, Kierkegaard distances himself from both. His more traditional approach has no use for such unorthodox distinctions as that between spirit and Nature in God. Nonetheless, on a human level he also interprets sinfulness as a removal from "spirit," a regression to a more "natural" synthesis of soul and body. For him the conscious acceptance of the primordial dependence introduces an eternal element into man's being and constitutes in it a spiritual self. Here especially one detects traces of Schelling's influence. For the German idealist the spiritual origin of freedom lies outside the succession of time, in a primary act that determines all time-and-space-conditioned activity. In Schelling's own words,

> The act whereby life in time is determined belongs itself not to time but to eternity. It does not precede life even with respect to time, but goes through time (without being grasped by it) as a by nature eternal deed. Through it human life reaches up to the origin of creation, because through it man is, outside the realm of creation, free and of eternal origin. However incomprehensible this idea may appear to common thinking, there nevertheless corresponds in each person a feeling to it, as if he had been from all eternity what he is, rather than having become so in time.[1]

Man is constituted as *act* and as *will* in his timeless origin, and this aboriginal being-act conditions all his activity in time. The impact of this theory upon Schopenhauer and, through him, upon Nietzsche is evident. But it also profoundly affected Kierkegaard's concept of the self as will. Beginning with *Either/Or* he consistently describes genuine selfhood as a *choice*. The self posits itself by choosing itself. Hence, freedom constitutes man's very essence.

> I choose the absolute, for I myself am the absolute, I posit the absolute and I myself am the absolute; but in complete identity with this I can say that I choose the absolute which chooses me, that I posit the absolute which posits me. . . . And what is the absolute? It is I myself in my eternal validity. (EO, 2:217-18)

In his later writings Kierkegaard qualifies the extent to which active self-realization has an absolute character. But the primacy of the will and the necessity of a moral choice remain essential conditions for establishing genuine selfhood. Later in *The Sickness Unto Death* he still asserts, "The more will, the more self. A man who has no will at all is no self" (SUD, 29-30). And in *Training in Christianity* the process of self-realization is once again defined as a choice of oneself (TC, 159). On the other hand, a corrective of what

---

[1]Friedrich Schelling, *Philosophische Untersuchungen über das Wesen der Menschlichen Freiheit*, in *Werke Auswahl in drei Bände*, ed. Otto Weisz (Leipzig: Eckchardt, 1907) 3:481-82.

would otherwise have remained a purely voluntaristic (and virtually atheistic) theory of self appears already in the "Ultimatum" at the end of *Either/Or*. There one learns that not the ethical choice alone establishes the self "in its eternal validity," but the awareness of the essential inadequacy of this choice, the idea that before God "we are always in the wrong." This inadequacy of the ethical realm is, of course, the principal theme of *Fear and Trembling* but also, in a somewhat different version (emphasizing failure rather than moral inadequacy), of *Repetition*.

The Eternal and the Temporal

Having acquainted oneself with the main source of Kierkegaard's theory of the self, one may now turn to his own discussion of the synthesis of the eternal and the temporal. This synthesis, both in *The Concept of Anxiety* and in *The Sickness Unto Death*, completes the immediate synthesis of soul and body, and establishes the self as spirit.

> Man is a synthesis of the psychical and the physical; however, a synthesis is unthinkable if the two are not united in a third. This third is spirit. (CA, 43)

It appears that "soul" (or "psychical") in this context (in contrast to its use in Kierkegaard's "religious" works) means no more than the animating principle that has the potential to become spirit but has to pass through a process of reflection in order to do so. It is a category of immediacy. John Elrod defines it well.

> To exist soulishly determined means to exist in accord with one's natural and cultural immediacy. It means living according to the categories of nature and culture totally devoid of an awareness of one's self as a self. But with the inflection of spirit, this soulish determination of the self in its natural and cultural immediacy becomes conscious of itself as real and ideal, is challenged by the possibility of its own freedom, and is stratified as a being which is in both time and eternity.[2]

---

[2]John W. Elrod, *Being and Existence in Kierkegaard's Pseudonymous Works* (Princeton: Princeton University Press, 1975) 40.

The spirit, "the third factor," constitutes in fact a new synthesis—between the eternal and the temporal—or, more correctly, it transforms the existing synthesis into a wholly different one.

> The synthesis of the temporal and the eternal is not another synthesis, but is the expression for the first synthesis, according to which man is a synthesis of psyche and body that is sustained by spirit. (CA, 88)

Nor does the dynamic opposition eternal-temporal exhaust the existential synthesis. In *The Sickness Unto Death* other dialectical poles appear—the finite and the infinite, the necessary and the possible. Though their dialectical oppositions do not appear in *The Concept of Anxiety*, Kierkegaard refers to these concepts in a manner wholly compatible with the later "synthesis." Since what is being dealt with here is a development rather than a change, I shall assume their presence in the overall synthesis and treat them (as well as the eternal-temporal) as partial "syntheses" even though, strictly speaking, there is only one synthesis. It may be asked whether they belong to the spiritualization process proper, or whether they form part of the "immediate" synthesis of body and soul. No doubt they belong to the spiritualization process proper, yet in such a way that they remain subordinate stages that do not receive their definitive meaning until the synthesis of the eternal and the temporal has been posited. The synthesis of the eternal and the temporal differs from the other two: spirit is identified with *one* of the elements of the synthesis, the eternal, while at the same time resulting from the supreme synthesis itself.[3]

> The synthesis of the psychical and the physical is to be posited by spirit; but spirit is eternal, and the synthesis is, therefore, only when spirit posits the first synthesis along with the second synthesis of the temporal and the eternal. (CA, 90-91)

The eternal, as such, introduces a transcendent dimension, absent

---

[3]Mark C. Taylor, in *Kierkegaard's Pseudonymous Authorship: A Study of Time and the Self* (Princeton: Princeton University Press, 1975) 88-89, has drawn attention to this apparent discrepancy.

from the previous categories, that wholly transforms the existing synthesis.

The "syntheses" of the infinite and the possible correspond roughly to those stages of the spiritualization process to which Kierkegaard elsewhere refers as aesthetic and ethical, while the concluding one of the eternal-temporal corresponds to the religious stage. The association remains approximate at any moment and ceases to apply altogether once the lower synthesis becomes transformed by the higher one: at that point the infinite and the possible become convertible with the eternal. But separately from the eternal they belong to a lower level of reflection.

In *The Concept of Irony* Kierkegaard had criticized the "infinity without finitude, an infinity void of content" (CI, 290). In doing so he had been influenced by Goethe's idea of *Humanität*, which, perhaps under the impact of Spinoza, united the finite and the infinite as necessary complements. Kierkegaard opposes the "mastered" irony based upon this integrated view to the typically romantic irony, "the infinite absolute negativity" expression of an infinite striving "wherein it turns riot" (CI, 63).

> When irony has been mastered in this way, when the wild infinity wherein it storms consumingly forth has been restrained, it does not follow that it should lose then its significance. . . . Irony now limits, renders finite, defines, and thereby yields truth, actuality and content. (CI, 338)

In calling for a synthesis of the finite and the infinite, Kierkegaard here adopts Hegel's schema without accepting its idealistic implications. Infinity thereby means not a divine predicate, but a quality of existence that allows the person to transcend his given situation. It is, in fact, an attribute of freedom. Wilhelm Anz argues that Kierkegaard has not always succeeded in limiting this subjective infinity and, hence, in properly distinguishing the divine and the human attribute.[4] This may well be true, but it should not overtly concern one. For, despite its idealist origins, Kierkegaard's notion of infinity marks a return to the more modest and

---

[4]Wilhelm Anz, *Kierkegaard und der deutsche Idealismus* (Tübingen: J. C. B. Mohr, 1956) 32-33.

mostly negative infinity of the Greeks—*to apeiron*—which, as Plato had argued, must be limited by *to peras* in order to constitute the real.[5] This dialectical moment of infinity is the work of the imagination, "the medium of the process of infinitizing" (SUD, 30). It constitutes the "expanding factor" in the self that enables it to move beyond the given and thereby to achieve the distance required for the reflection essential to the spiritualization process. But to the infinitizing movement must always correspond a finitizing one. The infinite, negative Idea "must again assert itself and render the Idea finite, make it concrete" (CI, 326).

Yet for Kierkegaard there is still another infinity than that of the imagination: the inwardly infinite, which is directly related to the self's religious nature. In *The Concept of Irony* he clearly distinguished the two.

> But infinity may be either an external or an internal infinity. The person who would have an infinitely poetical enjoyment also has an infinity before him, but it is an external infinity. When I enjoy I am constantly outside myself in the "other." But such an infinity must cancel itself. Only if I am not outside myself in what I enjoy but in myself, only then is my enjoyment infinite, for it is inwardly infinite. He who enjoys poetically, were he to enjoy the whole world, would still lack one enjoyment: he does not enjoy himself. To enjoy oneself (naturally not in a Stoic or egotistical sense, for here again there is no true infinity, but in a religious sense) is alone the true infinity. (CI, 313)

It is this religious infinity that Kierkegaard will more and more explore in his subsequent works—first in *Fear and Trembling*, in the so-called movement of infinity by which the religious person resigns his claim on the temporal. This movement precedes the act of faith that "by virtue of the absurd" reasserts its claim on the finite (FT, 79). Unlike Socrates, whose ignorance expressed infinite

---

[5]The ancients had, at least in late antiquity, also a positive idea of the infinite. Thus, for Epicurus the instant holds a fullness of content and an infinity of experience that renders immortality superfluous. The same idea appears in Marcus Aurelius. Indeed, the idea of the instant implies logically the idea of the infinite and excludes mere finitude. Cf. Rodolfo Mondolfo, *Problemi del pesiero antico* (Bologna: N. Zanichelli, 1935) 216-21, and *L'infinito nel pensiero dei Greci* (Florence: Le Monnier, 1934).

resignation, Abraham believed "and believed for this life" (FT, 34); "it is about the temporal, the finite, [that] everything turns in this [Abraham's] case" (FT, 60).

Here one detects how even the religious infinity has its dangers. It may carry the religious person away from himself and his earthly task into an attitude of mystical indifference toward the finite.

> The God-relationship is an infinitizing, but in fantasy this infinitizing can so sweep a man off his feet that his state is simply an intoxication. To exist before God may seem unendurable to a man because he cannot come back to himself, become himself. (SUD, 32)

Hence, man cannot unconditionally entrust himself even to the religious infinite, unless he balances his devotion by an appropriate concern for the finite. Only after it has become identical with the (religious) eternal does the infinite allow itself to be unqualifiedly pursued, because then it replaces its opposition to the finite by an integration with it. Nevertheless, the first, oppositional synthesis remains a necessary moment of reflection; without it the self would never move beyond the immediacy of the given.[6]

In establishing the synthesis of the possible and the necessary, the individual overcomes the purely aesthetic attitude in a new consciousness of freedom. Yet here again the temptation of the infinite awaits him, for he may reduce that freedom to a mere feeling of "infinite possibility." Kierkegaard, well aware of this danger, detaches himself from Schelling's theory of freedom, which collapses the possible and the necessary in their Ground. In contrast to the idealistic philosopher, he insists on a permanent dialectical opposition between the two poles. Without an awareness of its restricting finitude, that is, its necessity, the sense of freedom turns into an empty *feeling of possibility*. Like the Stoic consciousness in

---

[6]In assuming that the relation finite-infinite belongs already to the process of spiritualization proper, my reading differs from John W. Elrod's, for whom this relation refers to the same phenomenon designated by the soul-body duality (*Being and Existence*, 37). Still, Elrod himself mentions reflection as a "cooperative aspect of the process of infinitizing" (p. 34), while defining the soul-body relation as immediate, "totally devoid of an awareness of one's self as self" (p. 401).

Hegel's *Phenomenology of Mind,* it asserts its infinite potential only by means of a steadfast refusal of any concrete content. The polemics with Hegel, at their height in *Philosophical Fragments,* continue in *The Concept of Anxiety.* Nevertheless, Kierkegaard's firm rejection of the romantic concept of freedom marks a return to a Hegelian synthesis of the possible and the necessary. In *Philosophical Fragments* he had posited (against Aristotle) that the possible excludes the necessary, since it requires an additional determination to be actual. The process of *becoming* by which the transition from the possible to the actual is effected has a beginning and hence lacks the inability for nonexistence that characterizes genuine necessity. Now, in *The Concept of Anxiety,* he presents a different concept of possibility that, to be actual, *requires a combination with necessity* (Hegel's own definition).[7]

With awareness of freedom grows awareness of time. For the Greeks freedom had not yet become the essential category of man's self-understanding. Therefore, they also lacked a clear sense of time. "If Greek life in any way denotes any qualification of time, it is past time. However, past time is not defined in its relation to the present and the future but as a qualification of time in general, as a passing by" (CA, 89). The modern sense of freedom places the emphasis on the future. Kierkegaard contrasts it to the ancient recollection as "the category, namely repetition, by which one enters eternity forwards" (CA, 90). He thereby resumes the theory he had developed in *Repetition.*

> Just as they [the Greeks] taught that all knowledge is a recollection, so will modern philosophy teach that the whole of life is a repetition. . . . Repetition and recollection are the same movement, only in opposite directions, for what is recollected has been,

---

[7]The new compatibility of the possible with the necessary may well be due to its combination with the romantic infinite. "In possibility things are equally possible" (CA, 156); "He who is educated by possibility is educated in accordance with his infinitude" (ibid.). Such an "infinite possibility" requires a restriction (a "necessity" in a wholly different sense) to achieve the transaction to actuality. Cf. Nicola Abagnano, "Kierkegaard e il sentiero della possibilita, " in *Studi Kierkegaardiani,* ed. Cornelio Fabro (Brescia: Morcelliana, 1957) 9-28.

is repeated backwards, whereas repetition properly so called is recollected forwards. (R, 3-4)[8]

In such a remembrance of the past as permanent reality, the consciousness of time remains dormant. ("The Greeks did not in the profoundest sense grasp . . . temporality" [CA, 87].) Only an orientation toward the future fully awakens the sense of time.[9] Faced with an empty possibility to which he must give content, the individual experiences dread, the fear of nothingness. In this anxious confrontation with the future, he becomes clearly aware of his temporality. Anxiety becomes the very face of the future.

Kierkegaard wanted, above all, to establish the link between dread and time. Before writing *The Concept of Anxiety* he wrote in his diary, "It is quite possible to show that a very precise and correct usage of language links anxiety and the future together" (JP, 1:98). Yet the ultimate significance of this dread of the future consists in its projection of eternity. In it the subject unconsciously longs for spiritual selfhood. The *eternal* dwells in it as in its own projected shadow. In the indeterminacy of the future the subject hears the voice of spiritual transcendence calling it away from the immediate here-and-now and inviting it to pass from the temporal to the eternal reality. This encounter with the beyond threatens man's closed existence and hence frightens him.

> In order to go to the other, we must always move through a dark and narrow passage. Even if it is the good [which beckons us] at first it oppresses us. But the moment when the passage is narrowest and the anxiety most intense, it will appear—while we move from the *other* below us the nothingness of which attracts as well

---

[8]For a further development of the idea of repetition as the forward movement of freedom, cf. "Kierkegaard's Religion as Freedom," chapter 2 in my *A Dubious Heritage* (New York: Newman Books [Paulist Press], 1979) 30-52.

[9]Paul Tillich exactly paraphrases Kierkegaard's thought on the link between the two.

> It is the future that awakens us to the mystery of time. Time runs from the beginning to the end, but our awareness of time goes in the opposite direction. It starts with the anxious anticipation of the end. In the light of the future we see the past and the present.

The Eternal Now (New York: Scribner, 1963) 123. Mark Taylor brought this passage to my attention.

as frightens us, to the other above us, infinitely high, the absolutely *other* which also for the mind is a nothing—because of its excessive light.[10]

However, spiritual selfhood requires more than active self-realization. Active striving alone never comes to terms with its own ultimacy. It never confronts the absolute that it constantly assumes. Only in the religious attitude does the self achieve a conscious relation to that absolute that at once is the source of self-realization and transcends it. Kierkegaard identifies this transcendent element as *the eternal.* In it the self surpasses the pure succession of an ever-renewed forward movement that constantly asserts and relativizes its existence in time. The realized present ever again gives way to the possible future. In its relation to the eternal, however, the self attains that permanence that first fully constitutes selfhood in time. Here existence reaches back to that original point in which, according to Schelling, the self is "free beyond createdness and of eternal origin."[11] Even Kant felt the need to ground freedom in a unique deed that can be recognized only "through Reason independently of all conditions of time."[12] Yet neither Kant nor Schelling ever satisfactorily answered the question of how a self identical with the free deed can ever *transcend time.* How can what consists in an acting will ever surpass an unending (and hence timebound) pursuit of the possible? If the eternal has any place in such a theory, can it be more than that of an infinite possibility? One commentator, perhaps more consistent than others, has accepted this consequence, also for Kierkegaard. Enzo Paci writes,

> The act . . . is always in time and is never the atemporal and the absolute, no more than it is ever the elementary, the simple, the atomic, the one. Further, the "foundation" is never a real but a possible, never a being but the possibility of aperture of the becoming in the future. Precisely because actuality is always tem-

---

[10]Jean Wahl, *Études Kierkegaardiennes* (Paris: Vrin, 1974) 251.

[11]*Menschlichen Freiheit*, 482.

[12]*Die Religion innerhalb der Grenzen der reinen vernunft*, in *Werke* (Berlin: Preussische Akademie der Wissenschaften, 1900-1942) 6:31.

poral, spirit is possibility, freedom, rather than being and necessity.[13]

If the absolute is conceived of as a God, existing in and by itself, the idea of a necessary, fully real being must be replaced by that of a pure possibility. Paci believes this conclusion is implied in Kierkegaard's theory.

Such a closed interpretation of the self as free act hardly corresponds to what Kierkegaard had in mind. He was fully aware of the consequences involved in simply identifying selfhood with self-determination and thereby tying it to an insurmountable temporality. He also took measures to avoid them. For him the ultimate category or selfhood is not infinite *possibility*, which is indefinite openness, but *eternity*. Moreover, the category of eternity is not merely one element of a concluding synthesis, unlike the possible that appears as only *one* of the dialectical poles of a synthesis. The relation to the eternal that concludes the constitution of selfhood has no dialectical counterpart. But since this relation also penetrates all other temporal aspects of the self, the eternal must, *in addition*, establish a bipolar synthesis with the temporal. Without this final synthesis the eternal would simply abolish the temporal and suppress the entire process of free self-realization. Hence, the eternal, though clearly transcending the temporal, must also relate to it. It could not enter the existing synthesis without inserting itself into it as *one* of the two elements of a new synthesis. But it is the *eternal* alone that determines the self as spirit. Kierkegaard perceived the uniqueness of "the eternal," where Schelling, steeped in the romantic use (and abuse!) of religious language, had failed to grasp fully the distinctness of the eternal from the infinitely possible. To be sure, Kierkegaard's solution presents some problems of its own. Can a self defined as freedom still remain open to the eternal? Does the eternal not conflict with time? Is the relativity of actions accomplished in time through which man achieves his selfhood compatible with a relation to an absolute beyond time? Kierkegaard himself once raised the question: "Can the eternal be

---

[13]"Su due significati del concetto dell'angoscia in Kierkegaard," in *Symposium Kierkegaardianum, Orbis Litterarum X* (Copenhagen: Munksgaard, 1955) 199.

decided in time?" (JP, 4:4806). To answer it one must first clarify
the concept of time itself.

The Instant

Thus far the self-actualization of freedom has been assumed to
entail a complete concept of time, if not of eternity. But this is far
from being the case. Being primarily future-directed, the experience of duration implied in free self-actualization lacks the element
of permanence needed to retain the past and to anticipate the future in the present. Its constant forward movement, no more than
the ancient recollection, yields the sense of present that characterizes a complete experience of time. Only with the relation to the
eternal does time reach its fullness (JP, 4:4789). When the Eternal
entered the temporal at the moment of the Incarnation it transformed human time-consciousness.

> The pivotal concept in Christianity, that which makes all things
> new, is the fullness of time, but the fullness of time is the moment
> as the eternal, and yet this eternal is also the future and the past.
> (CA, 90)

To be sure, there always had to be some element of everlastingness, and hence at least an inkling of eternity in duration, for
that is the very condition of consciousness in general and of time-
consciousness in particular.

> If time is correctly defined as an infinite succession, it most likely
> is also defined as the present, the past, and the future. This dis-
> tinction, however, is incorrect if it is considered to be implicit in
> time itself, because the distinction appears only through the rela-
> tion of time to eternity and through the reflection of eternity in time.
> (CA, 85)

In that general sense all time-consciousness implies a notion of
permanence. But unless it is interpreted as an intersection of time
by eternity, this permanent element tends to be repelled to the past
or propelled into the future. The Greek eternity lies behind, as the
past "that can only be entered backwards" (CA, 90). As Kierkegaard has explained in *Philosophical Fragments* (published in the

same year as *The Concept of Anxiety*), Socratic recollection means more than reminiscing about historical events: the recollected past grounds one's present existence. Nevertheless, even though recollection transcends the past as mere past, it attains the eternal only in a temporal *image* that lacks the necessary nature of true eternity. Whatever comes into existence may be immutable once it exists, but it does not thereby become eternal. The immutability of the past annihilates the merely possible by becoming irreversible and thus excluding possible alternatives, but it never attains the intrinsic necessity of the eternal. In an early diary entry, Kierkegaard notes how, by a strange dialectic, the concentration on the past may turn into an expectation of the future, as in the Jewish mind (JP, 4:4788)—a precocious version of the exegetical principle *Urzeit ist Endzeit*.

The nature of the eternal implied in the ancient recollection may remain a matter of debate. But about the nature of its presence in the "modern" mind there can be no doubt. The indefinite future that receives all the emphasis contains unquestionably an image of eternity. Yet the eternal here appears only "incognito," that is, without a real present. The "present" merely functions as a dividing line between a closed past and an open future, without real content of its own. "As long as the instant is posited . . . merely as a *discrimen*, then the future is the eternal" (CA, 90). The subject remains in a dreaming state toward a spiritual existence that it conceives of only as substanceless project. "The eternal must not be understood merely as a denominator of *transitus* but also as a continuous state of fulfillment" (JP, 1:83).

In contrast to the Greeks and the "moderns," Christianity presents the eternal *as distinct from the temporal*. "Christianity continually speaks about eternity, constantly thinks about the eternal" (JP, 4:4799). It is true that Kierkegaard also attributes to it a preoccupation with the future, with "postexistence" as opposed to the preexistence or even the concern with the immediate present of the Greeks (JP, 5:5947). In *Repetition* he simply states that eternity for the Christian lies in the future, and in *Works of Love* he surprisingly denies that the contact between the eternal and the temporal occurs in the present, for reasons not unlike those used by the theologians of hope, namely, that the present itself would then be the eternal (which it obviously is not).

> If the eternal is in the temporal it is in the future (for the present cannot get hold of it, and the past is indeed past) or in possibility. The past is actuality; the future is possibility. Eternally the eternal is the eternal; in time the eternal is possibility, the future. Therefore we call tomorrow the future, but we also call eternal life the future. (WL, 234)

The emphasis on the future is justified insofar as Christianity first conceived of eternity as that endless openness that only the future possesses. In fact, the same idea lies at the origin of what Kierkegaard refers to as "the modern" attitude—however far it may since have removed itself from the Christian view. But unless one relates these statements about the eternal as future to the more fundamental emphasis on the *present* as the meeting point of time and eternity, they distort the perspective of Kierkegaard's theory. In an early edifying discourse, he explicitly defines the relation to the future as a subordinate one: "Through the eternal can one conquer the future, because the eternal is the foundation of the future" (ED, 1:21).

The eternal is the "fullness of time" (JP, 4:4789) that allows the present to incorporate past and future into its own everlastingness. As Kierkegaard formulates it in a Christian discourse:

> When by the help of eternity a man lives absorbed in today, he turns his back upon the next day, so that he does not see it at all. If he turns around, eternity is confused before his eyes, it becomes the next day. But if for the sake of labouring more effectually towards the goal (eternity) he turns his back, he does not see the next day at all, whereas by the help of eternity he sees quite clearly today and its task. . . . Faith turns its back to the eternal in order precisely to have this [the eternal] with him today. But if a man turns, especially with earthly passion, towards the future, then he is farthest from the eternal. (CD, 76-77)

In this passage is the whole complex dialectic of the present and the future with respect to the eternal in Christianity. The eternal lies, indeed, also in the future, but it can be attained only through an intensive consciousness of the present. It becomes most manifest in the lasting presentness that man experiences at the privileged moments of his existence. Thus, joy consists in being fully present to oneself, in truly "being today." "Joy is the present tense with the whole emphasis upon the *present*. Therefore it is that God is blessed, who eternally says, 'Today' " (CD, 350).

To the present-less time-consciousness of the Greeks and the moderns, Kierkegaard opposes the Christian awareness of the "instant," the point where time encounters the eternal.

> Time is, then, infinite succession; the life that is in time and is only of time has no present. In order to define the sensuous life, it is usually said that it is in the moment and only in the moment. By the moment, then, is understood that abstraction from the eternal that if it is to be present, is a parody of it. The present is the eternal, or rather, the eternal is the present, and the present is full. (CA, 86)

The *instant*, perhaps Kierkegaard's most original category, has nothing in common with the mathematical abstraction that divides a homogeneous line into past and future. In such a spatial representation no single moment has any particular significance. Nor does eternity consist in the infinite extension of such abstract "instants." "Eternity . . . is the opposite to the temporal as a whole" (CD, 103-104). At the same time only the eternal introduces a full awareness of time, thus positing both itself and its opposite: "eternity constantly pervades time" (CA, 89). This dual nature gives the eternal an ambiguous character. Viewed from time the instant passes from the past into the future; viewed from eternity it knows neither past nor future or, more correctly, it transforms past and future into a lasting present. Being an "atom of eternity" (CA, 88) the instant restructures the entire synthesis of selfhood into a spiritual one. "As soon as the spirit is posited, the moment is present" (CA, 88).

Only with the breakthrough of the eternal is the final synthesis of the self accomplished, the one that relates temporality as a whole to its opposite. "The synthesis of the psychical and the physical . . . is to be positied . . . only when the spirit posits the first synthesis along with the second synthesis of the temporal and the eternal" (CA, 90-91). To be sure, temporality was present from the beginning, and hence there was also an implicit consciousness of eternity. But once the eternal becomes conscious in its opposition to time, it entirely transforms the relation between present, past, and future. Through the eternal the present is posited "as the annulled succession" (CA, 86). The instant preserves the past and holds the spiritual essence of the future. Yet it forms no "eternal return," no mere repetition of the past in the future. It contains the past *as past*, in its unique and irreversible identity, and the future *as anticipated*, as what-is-yet-to-come and has never been. Far from abolishing history, the instant gives it an unprecedented importance: the moment of the objective presence of the eternal in time divides history into A.D. and B.C. Yet it overcomes the purely *successive* character of history. In the timeless instant all times and events acquire a lasting presence. In our age poets have expressed the same idea in different modes. Thus Claudel writes,

> *Rien n'a pu ou ne peut*
> *Être qui ne soit à ce moment même; toutes*
> *Choses sont présentes pour moi.*

(*La ville*)

And T. S. Eliot,

> *Or say that the end precedes the beginning,*
> *And the end and the beginning were always there*
> *Before the beginning and after the end*
> *And all is always now.*

("Burnt Norton" in *Four Quartets*)

Thus, "recollection" assumes a new meaning in the Christian context. Rather than denying history, it interiorizes time and thereby overcomes the distention of time through time.

Kierkegaard warns against a too easy "eternalization" of time or of any of its moments. Writing against Martensen and other Hegelians, he ridicules the idea of attaching to each moment an eternal significance *in its own right*. This idea, in fact, amounts to a simple divinization of time, which in the end abolishes the genuinely temporal. True eternity always retains a certain resistance to time, however much it permeates it. Hence, the birth of a new opposition (the eternal—the temporal) occurs once the eternal enters the soul-body synthesis. To treat each moment as it it were itself "immortal" (as, according to Kierkegaard, "metaphysics" does) reduces the eternalization of time to a "comic" level. The Christian concept of immortality evaluates time more realistically.

> Even though Christianity teaches that a person must render an account for every idle word he has spoken, we understand this simply as that total recollection. . . . Even though the teaching of Christianity cannot be more sharply illuminated by any opposite than that of the Greek conception that the immortals first drank of Lethe in order to forget, yet it by no means follows that recollection must become directly or indirectly comical—directly by recollecting ridiculous things or indirectly by transforming ridiculous things into essential decisions. (CA, 153-54)

Here the eternal clearly preserves an identity that never coincides with time or with any of its moments. Only in immortal life, that is, in existence after death, can eternity fully assert itself in the human spirit and this essential reality "will have the effect of the water of Lethe on whatever is unessential" (CA, 154). Kierkegaard's equation of pure eternity with immortality creates, however, serious problems. How can existence-in-time ever become *fully* "eternal"? The idea of immortality, constantly assumed, is never adequately treated in his work.

The difference between an existence locked in a closed temporality and one that has opened up to the eternal appears in the subject's attitude toward his own potential, and particularly in the concomitant feeling of anxiety. Each ascent to a more spiritual level of selfhood requires a leap into the unknown that provokes anxiety. Even the dormant awareness of possible selfhood that hides in the immediate harmony of soul and body elicits an unfocused dread. Such was the "profound, unexplained sorrow" (CA, 65) that clouded the ancient mind, an "anxiety before its own absence of anxiety."[14] Similarly, Kierkegaard describes man's condition before the Fall as anxious, even though neither a clear consciousness of freedom nor of eternity existed. Anxiety intensifies once freedom becomes fully conscious and the individual faces the gaping emptiness of his own fateful potential. Christianity alleviates this

---

[14]Jean Wahl, *Études Kierkegaardiennes*, 233.

dread before the future. The believer no longer realizes his freedom in a vacuum of sheer possibility, but in a present that preserves a redeemed past and maintains a continuity with the future.
Not the mere nothingness of infinite possibility confronts the
Christian, but the transcendent power to recapture (*Gjentagelse*—
"repetition"), ever again, a freedom disrupted through fate or sin.
Meanwhile, faith introduces its own anxiety. Once sinfulness has
been revealed, the ability to commit moral evil takes on a *concrete*
character unknown to the dreaming apprehension of the prelap-
sarian or pagan mind. The more the individual becomes aware of
his relation to the eternal, the more he realizes his ominous power
to sever that relation. Next to this dread before his power of evil,
the person who has confronted the eternal also experiences another, demoniacal fear of the good, the fear of admitting the eternal into his existence in time. If he yields to it, dread will turn into
despair (as described in *The Sickness Unto Death*).

The lesser or greater presence of the eternal determines the attitudes toward despair. The aesthetic attitude knows only an implicit despair, the refusal to let the spirit break through, which
Kierkegaard described in the behavior of a Nero (EO, 2:156) or even
of a young woman who dismisses the serious choices of life (*The
Sickness Unto Death*). The ethical attitude is perfectly capable of despair about the self as self-realizing project, but not of that ultimate
refusal to be oneself in one's relation to the eternal. Only in a clear
consciousness of the eternal can man fully choose closed finitude,
fatalistic resignation, deliberate escape into a world of fantasy, or
exclusive reliance on his own potential. The possibility of despair
presupposes a clear awareness of that full responsibility of existing
in time which man receives only in the light of eternity.

Comparing now the synthesis of the eternal and the temporal
with the other two syntheses, one notices that the former both
transcends and transforms the latter. In contrast to the balance between the finite and the infinite, between the necessary and the
possible, the final synthesis results in a clear priority of one term
(the eternal) over the other. The eternal, once it appears, transcends both its own synthesis (with time) and the two others. As
the principle that orders and structures the whole, the eternal has
no parallel. Indeed, it distorts the existing harmony in an upward

direction. The synthesis with the eternal is lopsided from the start: the temporal owes its own content to its opposite, and the eternal preserves its transcendence even after having posited its temporal counterpart. This imbalance also affects the other constituents of selfhood. The presence of spirit conveys a different dimension to the finite and the infinite than they had in the aesthetic or in the ethical attitudes. In a religious perspective the *infinite* becomes an attribute of the eternal, fully exchangeable with it. If one fails to keep this semantic shift in mind, one will object to the confusion of a term that signifies at once the realm of pure fantasy, unlimited human possibility, and the very nature of God. A similar transformation occurs in the possible. On a purely ethical level, the possible consists in that open-ended freedom that draws the individual beyond the circle of his given reality. It tempts him to the hazardous projects and fantastic schemes against which *The Sickness Unto Death* warned. But elsewhere the possible becomes synonymous with the eternal in man. Thus in *Works of Love*:

> The possibility of the good is more than possibility, for it is the eternal. This is the basis of the fact that one who hopes can never be deceived, for to hope is to expect the possibility of the good; but the possibility of the good is the eternal. (WL, 234)

And further:

> But if there is less love in him, there is also less of the eternal in him; but if there is less of the eternal in him, there is also less possibility, less awareness of possibility (for possibility appears through the temporal movement of the eternal within the eternal in a human being . . .). (WL, 241)

In *Fear and Trembling* and *Repetition*, Kierkegaard describes faith as the opening up of possibility. Even when fate appears to have closed off all avenues to an acceptable future, the knight of faith can still hope—and hope for this life—in virtue of the eternal. The coming of the eternal in time constitutes the ultimate possibility, for "with God nothing is impossible."

VI

The Socratic
Knowledge of God

by Robert C. Roberts

A striking feature of Kierkegaard's "stages" is the absence of any genuinely nonreligious viewpoint among them. Before examining the works most readers would expect the aesthetic and ethical stages to be forms of "secular humanism." But Judge William of *Either/Or* is a very religious man by any but the most stringent standards, and even the aesthete A does not seem to have any doubt about God's existence. A look at Kierkegaard's writings gives the impression that atheism was inconceivable to him. Indeed, he says, "but just as no one has ever proved [God's existence], so has there never been an atheist, even though there certainly have been many who have been unwilling to let what they knew (that the God exists) get control of their minds" (JP, 3:3606). He typically depicts Socrates as having a God-relationship: "let us never forget that

Socrates' ignorance was a kind of fear and worship of God, that his ignorance was the Greek version of the Jewish saying: the fear of the Lord is the beginning of wisdom" (SUD, 99). The purpose of the present essay is to explore and defend Kierkegaard's conception of the natural knowledge of God.

The Natural Knowledge of God

To "the Reason," Johannes Climacus argues in *Philosophical Fragments*, the God is "the Unknown" (PF, 49-54). The argument is part of an elaborate ironical deduction of the proposition that the God in time is the absolute paradox and the object of "the Reason's" paradoxical passion for its own downfall. But there is no reason to doubt that Kierkegaard himself believes this subconclusion: that no argument can shed any light on God's existence or nature.

The natural knowledge of God is not a product of inference, but of self-knowledge. "[God] is in the creation," says Johannes Climacus, "and present everywhere in it, but directly he is not there; and only when the individual turns to his inner self, and hence only in the inwardness of self-activity, does he have his attention aroused, and is enabled to see God" (CUP, 218). Judge William also describes such a moment of "self-activity": "So when all has become still around one, as solemn as a starlit night, when the soul is alone in the whole world, then there appears before one not a distinguished man, but the eternal Power itself. The heavens part, as it were, and the I chooses itself—or rather, receives itself" (EO, 2:181). What is such a moment like, and what does the soul have to acknowledge about itself to "see God" or stand in the presence of "the eternal Power itself"? To answer this question in at least one of the ways that Kierkegaard answers it, I shall focus on the chapter entitled "Anxiety as Saving through Faith" in *The Concept of Anxiety* (CA, 155-62), and a complementary section entitled "Necessity's Despair Is to Lack Possibility" in *The Sickness Unto Death* (SUD, 37-42).

In Kierkegaard's view, a person's ignorance of God (or disbelief in God) results not from a lack of information or evidence, but from a failure to know himself. And in adults this failure is always to some extent a matter of self-deception, of refusing to acknowledge things that are more or less before our eyes. Or, to put the matter a bit less moralistically, it is always a failure of imagination. He who is transparent to himself will not doubt that God exists, any more than the rest of us doubt that other people exist. Nor is he who is entirely clear that God exists capable of deceiving himself about the nature of his own life. The heavens' parting and the I's receiving itself are psychologically mutually implying. The passages from which I hope to receive some light on this claim are both concerned with the individual's apprehension of "possibility." God (or Providence) appears to the person who rightly and forthrightly reckons with "possibility."

The Anxiety of Possibility

Let us begin with the emotion that Kierkegaard calls "anxiety." An emotion can be thought of as a serious construal of one's circumstances and self in some way that impinges upon some active concern. If I am anxious, I construe my circumstances as insecure in some dimension in which I desire security. For example, if I seem to myself to be financially insecure, and I want to be financially secure, then I will be anxious about my finances. Both of these conditions—the construal and the desire—have to be in place for me to feel anxious. I can want financial security and be in fact financially insecure without feeling anxiety, if I do not *see* myself as financially insecure. Conversely, I can construe myself as financially insecure without feeling anxiety, if I don't *care* about financial security—perhaps I am a vagabond and have totally accepted not knowing where the next penny will come from. Also the *intensity* of my anxiety will be a function of two factors: how *much* I care about financial security and how insecure I construe myself to be. If I care a great deal about financial security but only see my situation as mildly insecure, my anxiety will be mild; if I see myself as very financially insecure, but am only mildly concerned about it, again my anxiety will be mild.

People vary in their susceptibility to financial anxiety. But the kind of anxiety that Vigilius Haufniensis describes as "saving through faith" is one to which every human being, in his view, is equally susceptible (unless a person has in fact come to faith through it). For there is no one who does not care about the kind of security on which this anxiety trades, and care about it very deeply; and there is no one whose objective insecurity would not be intolerable if he knew of it and if he did not rest in God. (What calls into question the universality of this susceptibility, in my opinion, is the difference between people's ability to *recognize* this insecurity; for highly intelligent people and people with a certain sort of upbringing [for example, like Kierkegaard's] seem to have more potential for recognizing it than others do. Self-deception is not the only obscuring factor here.) Haufniensis distinguishes "anxiety about men and finitudes" from "the anxiety of the possible" (CA, 157). Financial anxiety is a species of the former class, and its cure is either financial security or a disregard for the issue. Anxieties about men and finitudes can in principle be dispelled by a rearrangement of the men and finitudes in question. By contrast there is, according to Kierkegaard, no cure for the anxiety of the possible, short of resting in Providence. What is the anxiety of the possible?

Only the anxiety of possibility, says Haufniensis, "is through faith absolutely educative, because it consumes all finite ends and discovers all their deceptiveness" (CA, 155). What are "finite ends," and what is their "deceptiveness"? Finite ends are the means by which we seek to satisfy our passions for a secure identity and place in the world: they are such things as job, income, health, respect of peers, possessions, connections in the world of affairs, one's character and patterns of behavior, achievements, abilities, and so forth. And their deceptiveness is that all these means of security are themselves insecure: every one of them can be taken away or rendered ineffectual in a twinkling of an eye, either by a moral fall or by forces beyond one's control. The anxiety of possibility vividly sees the possibility of loss in all these "securities" by reckoning courageously and seeing the world as it is. This is not an anxiety about the loss of any one means of security (that would be an anxiety about men and finitudes). It is, indeed, an apprehension of the insecurity in the realm of "men and finitudes" *as a whole.*

When the "spiritless" person is anxious about this or that, he always reckons that there is some chance that the finitude in question will not be lost, or that if it is lost, it may be restorable or replaceable by something else. Haufniensis calls this attitude "shrewdness," and the eternal Power does not appear before a person who so thinks. The anxiety of possibility causes shrewdness to become "helpless and its most clever combinations vanish like a witticism" (CA, 161). When this happens, the self is confronted with a clear choice—either to "receive itself" or to slip back into the self-deceptive modes of thought from which it has briefly emerged in anxiety. If it receives itself, it comes into a relationship with Providence—that is, the eternal Power appears before it, and it entrusts itself to this Power rather than to the deceptive finite ends. The attribute of God that comes to light through the anxiety of possibility is his trustworthiness. The individual who emerges from this anxiety into "faith" has no specific promises, of course, but he does know this much: God is steady, strong, and benignly inclined toward him. In each of these ways God is to be contrasted with the deceptive finite ends.

The Despair of Necessity

The second contrasting pair of attitudes is despair/hope. In ordinary language, despair is hopelessness. This definition is narrower than that of Anti-Climacus in *The Sickness Unto Death,* where despair is defined as the unwillingness to be oneself as a synthesis of the finite and the infinite, the necessary and the possible, the temporal and the eternal. But of course, hopelessness is a form of unwillingness to be oneself if the self is so defined, for to be without hope is to understand oneself as having no way out, no alternatives, no "possibility." It is with despair as hopelessness, this despair that is closest to what we usually designate by the word, that we now have to do.

Not all the forms of despair that Anti-Climacus surveys are emotions, it seems. But this despair, like the anxiety just discussed, is an emotion—that is, a construal of the subject's situation and self in a way that impinges on some concern of the subject. (This is not to say it is necessarily a *conscious* state—the "philistine-bourgeois mentality" [SUD, 41f.] is a largely unconscious hopelessness—for both concerns and construals can be unconscious.) Despair surfaces when "a person is brought to his extremity, when, humanly speaking, there is no possibility" (SUD, 38). But of course, the concern that makes his situation for him a situation of extremity has to be nonnegotiable, for if he could just back off from the concern by resignation, then there would a "way out" for him after all, and his emotion would only have *seemed* to be despair. A child, for example, may feel that "the world will come to an end" if he does not get the piece of candy he wants; but he soon finds that his interests change, and his "despair" is relieved. And adults succeed daily in handling their emotions by managing their desires and concerns—by learning not to *want* things that are out of reach, and by learning to mitigate their concerns for the objects of their disappointments. By contrast, the concern that is the basis of real despair has to be untouchable by the methods of stoicism.

So this concern must be a basic one, such as the concern for self-esteem, or for meaning or fulfillment. And now the person who is "brought to his extremity" is one who sees that, "humanly speaking, there is no possibility" of satisfying this nonnegotiable concern. Like Qoheleth, he sees that from the earthly perspective there is no way of attaining this sine qua non. All is vanity. But even Qoheleth is not quite at his extremity, for he poetizes his despair (one gets the impression), so that the full actuality of his situation does not bear in upon him in realistic insight. And besides that, he finds relief in the immediate: "So I saw that there is nothing better than that a man should enjoy his work, for that is his lot; who can bring him to see what will be after him?" (Eccles. 3:22) So unlike Qoheleth, the person who is brought to his extremity does not mitigate his impression of hopelessness either by poetizing or by mendacious self-immersion in the immediate. When he refuses all false comfort, and cannot get loose from this demand of his nature (for the possibility of self-esteem, meaning, or some other necessary condition of selfhood), and sees that all of finitude is vanity with respect to this demand, "then only this helps: that for God everything is possible" (SUD, 39).

"[I]n despair his soul's despair fights to be permitted to despair, to attain, if you please, the composure to despair, to obtain the total personality's consent to despair and to be in despair" (SUD, 38). The self that is on the verge of becoming transparent to itself is torn between its honesty and its comfort. Its honesty presses it toward despair (that is, despair of finding satisfaction in the finite), but since its demand is nonnegotiable, it cannot despair as honesty demands unless it can find the "composure" to despair—that is, some way of satisfying its nonnegotiable demand for possibility that will permit it to despair over the fact that the finite offers it no possibility. Consequently, the moment in which it comes to believe that with God all things are possible and the moment in which it honestly despairs of finding the required possibility in the finite, are the same moment. Self-transparency begets the God-relationship, and the God-relationship begets self-transparency. The attributes of God that come to light through the despair of necessity are his benevolence and his eternity.

There is a seeming incongruity between the God who comes to light through the despair of necessity and the God who comes to light through the apprehension that, if we have only the finite to go to, *too much* is possible. The answer to this insecurity, accordingly, is a God with whom *not* all things are possible, a God who can be *trusted*. The despair of necessity, on the other hand, is the apprehension that the finite offers *too little* possibility, and so the answer to it is a God with whom all things are possible. But this incongruity is only an appearance created by words. For when Anti-Climacus says that for God all things are possible, he surely does not mean to include the possibilities of God's being malevolent or undependable. Jointly, the anxiety and the despair examined here bring to light a God who is benevolent and trustworthy and eternal, and whose power transcends all the contingencies of earthly life.

Deterministic Suffocation

The third set of contrasting attitudes about possibility is deterministic suffocation/freedom. Unlike the first two sets, this one does not contain emotions, at least not any that have names in ordinary language. Also unlike anxiety and despair, deterministic suffocation does not bring God's *existence* to light. Instead, assuming that God is known to exist, the unacceptability of determinism to the self brings to light something about God's *nature*.

Determinism[1] is the belief that the course of the future is already set—determined—as if on tracks of steel. That is, the commonsense belief that there are *possibilities* of future events (including human actions) is false. For if determinism is true, then there are no events that *may* happen, but only some that *will* happen and others that *will not*. Given the present state of the world and that the causal laws governing it are inviolable, the events that will happen cannot not happen, and those that will not happen cannot happen: everything happens by causal necessity.

If this is true, then in an ethically important sense, human beings are never responsible for anything they do. One must distinguish between two applications of the word *responsible*. A person is responsible for her actions in an ethical sense when it is appropriate to hold her responsible for them—to praise her if they are good and condemn her if they are bad. She is responsible for her actions when they redound to *her* moral credit or discredit. In

---

[1]Anti-Climacus uses the words *determinist* and *fatalist* indifferently but intends, I believe, the doctrine that contemporary philosophers know as determinism, not the one we would call fatalism. Fatalism is the view that there are some events that are going to happen *no matter what else happens*, but determinism only claims that whatever happens has sufficient causal antecedents. Thus, for example, if my dying on a certain day in an automobile wreck were fatalistically determined, that event would occur no matter what I did to prevent it. But for it to be merely determined, it is only required that there be a set of antecedent conditions such that, given them, it could not not occur; and that each of these in turn have a set of antecedent conditions such that given them it could not not occur, and so forth back to the origin of the world. Since various decisions of my own are events in this series, it is not the case that nothing I might have done would have prevented my death on this day. If, for example, I had chosen to take the bus to work on this day, I would not have died in that accident. But it must be noted that for the determinist there is something odd about the notion of something that I "might have done." For given the causal antecedents of my choice to take the car on that day, there was no possibility that I might have chosen to take the bus. We can imagine this "possibility" and talk about it, but if determinism is true, then it must be strictly empty, not a real possibility. For me to have chosen to take the bus on that day, the world would have had to have a different history than it had.

another sense of the word, we speak of nonpersons as responsible for events. An avalanche can be responsible for destroying a village, a tree responsible for disturbing the flow of electricity into a house, dioxin in a lake responsible for an increased incidence of cancer in a community. In such cases being responsible for an occurrence does not redound to the moral credit or discredit of the "agent," nor is there any sense in which the "agent" can take credit or blame for the occurrence. Now it is plausible to think that one essential difference between the moral and the nonmoral applications of *responsible* is this: A person can be held *morally* responsible for an action only if the occurrence in question to some degree *originates* with *her*, that is to say, only if antecedent conditions of the individual's choice are *not* sufficient for its occurrence. And it is precisely because when "agents" like avalanches, trees, and dioxin "do" things, there exist or may exist antecedent conditions such that, given them, the occurrences could not not occur, that we do not credit the "agent" with the occurrence. The "agent" in such cases is *only* a link in a causal chain, and in no sense an originator of one.

If this account is true, then the determinist, in giving up the belief that there are genuine possibilities, will also have given up the *moral* concept of responsibility. That is, there will be no morally significant difference between the "agency" of a human agent, and the "agency" of chemical and other agents. Human agents (or more precisely, occurrences in them such as desires and choices) will be nothing but links in the causal chain; they will not be originators of anything. Not that the determinist will be compelled, or even tempted, to cease using the moral concept of responsibility. He may find that talking in its terms is an indispensable tool for determining other human beings' behavior, perhaps even essential for keeping society on an even keel. The determinist is not committed, in consistency, to stop using the concept of moral responsibility, but only to cease believing that he or anyone else has moral responsibility.

Correlatively, the determinist is not committed to cease believing that he has options, but only to cease believing that he has morally significant options, or what one might call, from the point of view of moral personhood, genuine options. It is probably a practical impossibility to cease believing that we have options, but only a very strenuous difficulty to cease believing, with full transparency, that we have genuine options. The lucid determinist believes that he has options in the sense that his desires and decisions have causal efficacy; what he does not believe is that the events determined by his desires and decisions could, given the Big Bang (or whatever), be other than they will be. That is, he does not believe that by his desires and decisions and actions he authors himself or anything else in even the slightest way; all authorization of himself is outside himself in the past. It is this fact about determinism that violates the concept of a person. The stronger our sense of moral self-respect, the greater the sense of suffocation we will have if we become lucid believers in determinism.

If God exists, and determinism is true, then God is the ultimate determiner of all events, including one's actions. His will is identical to what actually happens. But if so, then his will is not something to which one can responsibly respond. On the other hand, if determinism is not true, then the will of God is not necessarily identical to what happens, and the relation between him and an individual can be one of personal interaction, in which the individual takes responsibility. In this case God's will is in part an ideal to which one is challenged to conform oneself.

But this question about the nature of God's will has momentous consequences for selfhood. As Anti-Climacus puts it, "the self of the determinist cannot breathe, for it is impossible to breathe necessity exclusively, because that would utterly suffocate a person's self" (SUD, 40). It is essential to personhood to take responsibility for oneself, to have some say in what one becomes. Anti-Climacus expresses this fact of high-moral common sense by calling the self a relation that relates *itself* to itself: The idea of a person who is a mere receptacle or transmitter of events, but not in any sense an originator of them, is for an ethical outlook self-contradictory.

So one might express the present theological implication of self-knowledge as follows: Self-knowledge brings to light that God is a person *inter*acting with human persons, and is not a total determiner of events in his creation, who only acts upon us. His will is not just necessity, but also possibility. "That God's will is the possible makes me able to pray" (SUD, 40).

Now most determinists are like most skeptics: They are at their best when lecturing or writing. When the skeptic turns to drinking coffee with companions, his epistemic tentativeness tends to dissipate. He converses and interacts with them just as though he *knew* they were there, sitting in front of him as big as life! When one of them insults him, the flush on his face and the rage in his eye betray that he is *sure* he's been insulted—as certain of it as your naivest realist. And in like manner, the ethical determinist is best at denying that he has options when he has no moral decisions to make. But as soon as a decision has to be made, his inconsistency comes out, and he takes the world to be as full of genuine options as the next fellow. He acts not like a determinist, but like a person.

Among people with a strong sense of moral personhood, real determinists (as opposed to lecturers on determinism) are a great rarity. For determinism entails keeping vividly before one's mind in at least some moments of significant action the conviction that one has no genuine options,[2] that everything one will do is deter-

---

[2]A colleague of mine has challenged this premise as follows: We are not obliged, on pain of self-deception, to keep before our mind with complete vividness truths that, via irrational emotions, disable us. We are rationally justified in turning our attention away from such truths in certain circumstances. He illustrates: A person has an irrational fear of spiders but must, to change the filter on his air conditioner, consort with the little critters in the crawlspace under his home. Once he has satisfied himself that his fear is irrational, he is rationally justified in focusing his attention on things other than the spiders as he crawls under the house. True, the spiders are there and he knows it; but he doesn't have to keep before his mind all the truths he knows to qualify as an honest man. Analogously someone who has satisfied himself by philosophical investigation that determinism is true will consider the debilitation of his agent-humanity, which comes from focusing on the truth of determinism, as an irrational factor in his mental makeup; the correct response to it may just be to divert his attention from the truth of determinism whenever he is required to act.

In response I would make the following three observations: Since giving a lecture on determinism is presumably itself a responsible act, adoption of this strategy would seem to preclude focusing on the truth of determinism even while attending most seriously to the truth of determinism—which seems an odd position to be in. Second, the belief in determinism would seem to be a very fundamental one to a person's view of himself and the world, rather unlike the truth

mined by events that occurred before one was born. Most "determinists" do not even try to apply their doctrine in consciousness, and it is for this reason that they do not feel the personal suffocation that the doctrine entails. But if a theoretical determinist were honestly to try this, then, according to Anti-Climacus, he would be driven to a kind of personal desperation analogous to the anxiety and despair examined here. He would discover a need as pressing in personal terms as the need to breathe is in physical terms. Indeed, he would find that determinism is an *impossibility* for him, as impossible as trying to hold his breath indefinitely. And if he is also clear that God exists, then this experience will show him the personal impossibility of believing that God's will is the necessary.

The Natural Generation of the Concept of God

So Kierkegaard's claim is that self-knowledge yields knowledge of God. "The true autodidact is precisely in the same degree a theodidact" (CA, 162). This claim raises a couple of questions. The first has to do with where the concept of God comes from. For if knowing God implies having a concept of God, and a person is supposed to be able to know God simply by knowing himself, it would seem that in some cases the self-knower would also have to be able to generate the concept of God out of his self-knowledge. Is this possible? And the second question has to do with the propriety of Kierkegaard's way of characterizing this knowledge of God. At least part of the time, he speaks as though the person experiences God's presence in the context of self-knowledge. But is this really what happens? Is it not rather that the individual comes

---

that spiders live under the house; and acting is a fundamental need of human life, rather unlike the need to change one's air conditioning filter. So the irrational factor in the mental makeup of the moral determinist is fundamental and pervasive in a way that the irrational fear of spiders is not. And third, going along with the second point, the potential friction created by conjoining fear of spiders and the acknowledgment of spiders is in principle curable and, at any rate, a feature accidental to the human condition; but the friction between the truth of determinism (if it is true) and the moral conception of a person is not susceptible to any imaginable medical treatment.

to realize his need for God (of for a God with certain characteristics), and then postulates God as an object of belief that satisfies this perceived need?

One can distinguish two kinds of experience of God, mediated and unmediated. A mediated experience will be one in which God is experienced through or in some other experience. For example, I may see God's glory reflected in a daffodil. I see the flower, but I see it not only under the concept *flower*, but also under the concept *product of the mind of God*. I do not experience a flower unless I construe the object before me as a flower, and I do not experience the glory of God in it unless I construe it as a product of the mind of God. Generally, it seems to be true of perceptual experiences that they are also conceptual: percepts without concepts are blind. But not all experiences of God are mediated, that is, they are not all perceptual. I also sometimes experience God simply by reflecting upon him ("contemplating" him). If in my anxiety I construe God as trustworthy, or in despair as the possibility of fulfillment for my life, there may be no perceptual object that gets construed in terms of a concept. I simply turn my attention (or have my attention turned) to God's trustworthiness and goodness.

In some experiences of God, then, there will be *perception*, and in others none. But there is no experience of God apart from the *concept* of God. And this returns one to the first question. For Kierkegaard's claim is that God can be known to anyone who can know himself in certain very general ways. But is this true for people who have not been taught a minimal concept of God? What if a person grows up in a culture that has no concept of God? If such a person reckons honestly enough with himself to begin to experience the anxiety of possibility or the despair of necessity, can he go on to "rest in Providence"? This much seems clear: he cannot do so unless there arises out of his experience also the concept of Providence. And so the question is whether a person, merely by being brought to his extremity in self-knowledge, could generate the concept of God?

Though it seems unlikely, I do not see anything impossible about it. After all, the concept of God had to be generated somewhere, and imaginative people generate concepts all the time. So there is nothing intrinsically problematic about a person, approaching the extremity of self-knowledge, coming up with the concept of an eternal trustworthy Benevolence beyond the realm of flux. I am not saying that such a person would sit down, like somebody writing a philosophy paper, and use his ingenuity to come up with the idea of something a relationship with which would satisfy his deepest psychological needs. More likely, the idea would just occur to him "spontaneously" as many of our ideas seem to do. And if it did occur to him, the idea of this transcendence might give him enough composure to go on and despair thoroughly of the finite, and thus to receive his self from God. I suppose it goes without saying that a person who already has a more or less correct concept of God in his "repertoire" (for example, a person who grows up in Christendom or Judaism or Islam) is enormously advantaged, in the matter of coming to know God, over someone who initially has no concept of God. Johannes Climacus seems to wonder whether the natural knowledge of God was ever in fact exemplified in paganism: " . . . of religiousness A one may say that, even if it has not been exemplified in paganism, it could have been, because it has only human nature in general as its assumption . . ." (CUP, 496). At other points, as I have noted, Kierkegaard seems quite certain that Socrates exemplified this religiousness.

Vigilius Haufniensis admits that anxiety of possibility does not always lead to faith, even when the individual does not mendaciously turn away from it: "I will not deny that whoever is educated by possibility is exposed to danger . . . , namely, suicide. If at the beginning of his education, he misunderstands the anxiety, so that it does not lead him to faith but away from faith, then he is lost" (CA, 158f.). And one might speculate that sometimes when this happens, it is because the individual, for one reason or another, does not bring the concept of Providence into play for himself. The reason might be that he does not have a concept of Providence available to him, and does not generate one in the course of his anxiety. Or it might be that he has something like the concept of Providence, but it is so distorted that it cannot meet his psychological needs, and yet is close enough to the concept to keep it from occurring to him that God is the answer.

The Immediacy
of the Natural Knowledge of God

The second question concerns the immediacy of the experience of God that occurs in the extremity of self-knowledge. That is, Kierkegaard seems to suggest that God is here not merely a postulate for belief, but that he appears to the individual, that the self-knower knows God with something like the immediacy of perception. Kierkegaard is quite clear that God is not known by inference. In *Philosophical Fragments*, chapter 3, Johannes Climacus offers some cavalier and rather unconvincing arguments to show that it is impossible to prove God's existence. But one gets the impression that even if he were shown an undeniably sound and informative argument for God's existence he would still deny that it yielded knowledge of God, simply because such knowledge was inferential. Essential to the knowledge of God is that it is fellowship, interaction, presence. Consequently, Kierkegaard would seem just as ready to reject, as yielding knowledge, pragmatic arguments of the form

1. People have need N for God.
2. Needs like N justify beliefs under conditions C.
3. C obtain in the religious case.
   Therefore we are justified in believing in God.

as he is to reject arguments that offer evidence or conceptual considerations in favor of God's existence.

But now the question is this: How can self-knowledge yield anything more than an impulse to postulate God as an object of belief? How can it yield a meeting with God? To answer this question, one needs to do two things: one must reckon with the epistemic peculiarities of meeting God in experience, and one must appreciate the similarity between the knowledge of God and other knowledge to which we are pressed by "psychological" exigency.

"No one has ever seen God," declares the evangelist (John 1:18), and one can extend this observation to the other senses. We do, of course, speak of seeing God, and of hearing him and touching him and tasting him. Later in the same gospel, Jesus says to Philip, "He who has seen me has seen the Father" (14:9). It appears that one thing such expressions are meant to indicate is that we do not just know *about* God (perhaps in the way we know about theoretical entities like protons); we also *meet* him, experience him. But still, this meeting is not a meeting in sense-experience. I see God's glory *reflected* in the daffodil, but the glory of the daffodil (which I *do* see with my eye) and the glory of God are different glories. And Jesus did not say, "He who has seen my body has seen the Father." Perhaps he meant something more like "He who has experienced my love and my authority has 'seen' the Father." But again, although one can "see" love, it is, unlike the glory of the daffodil, not an object of sense-experience. Perhaps one could say that it is an object of contemplation.

When we meet God, we meet him as an object of contemplation. We meet him as a personal presence, but as one from whom any sense-experiences that we may be having are usually quite remote. If we are heavily influenced by empiricism, we may be inclined to think it impossible to have an experience that has no sensory or imaginal "content." We may think that any knowledge that is very remote from sense-experience must be theoretical, inferential, indirect. But religious people will know that this is not true. Part of the reason for this is in the concept of God. For it is part of the concept of God that he is present. So to focus attention on God is to focus attention on a person in whose presence I live. If I succeed in focusing my attention on God (or he succeeds in turning my attention to himself), this focus of attention will be a meeting. Kierkegaard claims that this meeting happens, almost necessarily, in the extremity of self-knowledge. One can understand better how this knowledge of God can arise out of psychological exigency if one considers the similarity between it and our knowledge of *human* persons.

The Knowledge of God
and the Pressure of Actuality

We know that other people exist because we meet them daily. We depend upon them; they make appeals to us; they protest when we offend them; they please us, anger us, puzzle us, and many other things. But Pyrrhonistic skeptics claim they are not sure whether there are any other people. They think the grounds for our "belief" that there are other people are not strong enough to warrant a knowledge claim. But to say that I only believe others exist makes it sound as though my wife and children are objects of speculation for me, or the content of a hypothesis. However, for me it is not a hypothesis that my wife and children exist; after all, they are with me every day. In fact, I find that when my children are making requests of me, giving me kisses, producing dirty diapers, and the like, it is next to impossible to be epistemically tentative about their existence. I can imagine situations or states of mind in which I might become tentative about their existence—for example, some psychotic states of mind or a situation of extended separation without communication. But in the normal state of mind, and in the situation of interaction, tentativeness about other people's existence is next to impossible.

Kierkegaard might say that the compellingness in the psychological situation of the extremity of self-knowledge is analogous to the compellingness in the normal psychological situation of interaction with other human beings. Just as in the latter case a person cannot be tentative about the existence of other people, so a person who is lucid about himself cannot be tentative about the existence of God. The self-knower does not *believe* that God exists, anymore than I, in a moment of intense conversation with my wife, believe that she exists. The self-knower does not postulate God's existence; he stands in God's presence. God's existence is for him not a hypothesis, not even a tenaciously adhered to hypothesis; it is a certainty. If there are not many people for whom the existence of God is such a certainty, it is because there are not many who know themselves.

An Existentialist Objection to Kierkegaard

Let us end by looking at an existentialist objection to Kierkegaard's account of the natural knowledge of God. The existentialist will say that God is not the only, or even the best, answer to the extremity of self-knowledge, since the individual can find an end to his anxiety and hopelessness by an experience of the benignness of the Void. Indeed there is something rather childish and egoistical in the "Socratic" unwillingness to accept one's utter nothingness, this hankering after a personal relationship with the eternal, this yearning for immortality. It is more radical, more humble, and after all more realistic to find the solution to hopelessness *in* hopelessness and the solution to insecurity *in* insecurity. When, in the extremity of self-knowledge, one simply lets oneself be void, then it is not the eternal Power that appears before one, but something even better happens: Nothingness puts on a friendly face.

The last pages of Albert Camus's *The Stranger* appear to be an apologetic for this position. Meursault has been condemned to death by guillotine for murdering an Arab and is awaiting the day. He is obsessed with the idea of a loophole, of some possibility, however remote, of avoiding the inevitable—the possibility of a malfunction of the equipment or some way of escaping at the last minute, even if only to be shot in the back. Or the possibility of an appeal. He indulges in fantasy about "being an onlooker [at the execution] who comes to see the show, and can go home and vomit afterwards" and about framing "new laws, altering the penalties. What was wanted, to my mind, was to give the criminal a chance, if only a dog's chance; say, one chance in a thousand."[3] At one such moment of reflection, the chaplain, whom Meursault has repeatedly refused to see, comes in uninvited. In vain he tries a number of strategies for getting Meursault interested in God, but only succeeds in so estranging him that he starts hurling insults at the priest while gripping him by the neck of his cassock. Through this act of violent self-expression, Meursault not only seals the inevitability of the guillotine, but also gets reconciled to it. The jailers rescue the priest from Meursault's grip, and when they have all left Meursault falls asleep. When he awakes the stars are shining down on his face.

---

[3]Albert Camus, *The Stranger*, trans. Stuart Gilbert (New York: Random House, 1946) 138, 139.

Then, just on the edge of daybreak, I heard a steamer's siren. People were starting on a voyage to a world which had ceased to concern me forever. Almost for the first time in many months I thought of my mother. And now, it seemed to me, I understood why at her life's end she had taken on a "fiancé"; why she'd played at making a fresh start. There, too, in that Home where lives were flickering out, the dusk came as a mournful solace. With death so near, Mother must have felt like someone on the brink of freedom, ready to start life all over again. . . . It was as if that great rush of anger had washed me clean, emptied me of hope, and, gazing up at the dark sky spangled with its signs and stars, for the first time, the first, I laid my heart open to the benign indifference of the universe.[4]

Meursault's attitude could be called crisis stoicism or defense-mechanism stoicism. Unlike the traditional stoic, he does not undertake a long-term discipline of resigning himself to inevitabilities—he is far too passive a character for that—and yet the psychological result is similar. The universe is indifferent to him, but that indifference is painful only so long as he demands individual significance; if he can bring himself (or be brought) to give up that demand, then by comparison with the frustration it formerly caused him, the universe begins to appear tender and benign. Meursault finds relief in "identifying" with the indifference of nature, in giving up his enthusiasm for life—or at least for this individuality that he himself is. Apart from his laziness, Meursault is an excellent candidate for stoicism even from the beginning of the novel. For he is carried along quite passively on the tide of his social and physical environment; he has no passions, no focused, long-term interests or goals that would set him apart from the given world around him. Thus, he has no definition as a self, no integrity. As regards being an "individual" in Kierkegaard's sense, he is at the opposite extreme from Socrates. What little passion he does have is momentarily pressed out of him when he is condemned to death, and it is this minimal affirmation of individuality that grounds the anxiety and despair with which he is seen struggling in the last pages of the book.

---

[4]Ibid., 153-54.

The stoic strategy is, no doubt, one way some people get relief
from anxiety and despair without having an experience of God. But
I don't think that it constitutes an exception to Kierkegaard's claim
that knowledge of God supervenes upon the individual in the extremity of self-knowledge. This is not because Meursault is dishonest to himself about his situation, but because he has
suppressed the integrating passion for his individual life that is a
necessary condition of his *having* a self. With Kierkegaard's insistence on the necessity of individual self-concern to the formation
of the self, he must consider stoicism as a form of spiritual suicide
or attempted suicide. It makes sense that a self that is dead through
stoicism cannot be in the extremity of self-knowledge, even if it is
lucid about the insecurity of life, the meaninglessness of human
endeavor, and the inevitability of death. But if the word *suicide* is
used for what the stoic does to himself, Kierkegaard will insist that
the stoic cannot get beyond the attempt. The self's enthusiasm for
its own individuality is not something it can do away with: "The
person in despair cannot die; 'no more than the dagger can slaugh-
ter thoughts' can despair consume the eternal, the self at the root
of despair, whose worm does not die and whose fire is not
quenched" (SUD, 18). So the stoic's "suicide" is in the last analysis
a form of self-deception: not about his worldly prospects, but about
what he really wants out of life. He may think that he has conformed his will to nature, but if he could see his way clear to real
hope, he would drop his stoicism and immediately take hold of that
hope.

VII

Language and Freedom: Kierkegaard's Analysis of the Demonic in The Concept of Anxiety

by Ronald L. Hall

Kierkegaard insisted that one can enter an existence of faith only by concretely affirming one's radical individuality and freedom before God. Some have thought that Kierkegaard's unbridled praise for the individual, coupled with his disdain for "the crowd," drove him too far in the direction of an individualism that would finally lead him to deny what seems to be an obvious and *essential* element in the life of faith, namely, its social or communal component. One critic who has charged Kierkegaard with this kind of radical individualism is Professor Mark C. Taylor.[1] This essay is in-

---

[1]*Kierkegaard's Pseudonymous Authorship: A Study of Time and the Self* (Princeton: Princeton University Press, 1975) and *Journeys to Selfhood: Hegel and Kierkegaard* (Berkeley: University of California Press, 1980).

tended to be a response to Professor Taylor and a defense of Kierkegaard against the charge that he gave no essential place to the communal dimension in the life of faith.

The starting point in this venture is a small section of Kierkegaard's *The Concept of Anxiety* entitled "Anxiety about the Good (the Demonic)" (CA, 118-54). A close examination of this section of text will reveal that Professor Taylor (and other like-minded critics) is mistaken in his charge that Kierkegaard failed to give an essential place to the communal component in the life of faith. The key to Professor Taylor's mistake is his failure to recognize the role that Kierkegaard gives to *language* in the life of faith. Because language presupposes a social and communal context, if one could show that Kierkegaard allocates an essential place in the life of faith to language, it would show, I believe, that Kierkegaard allocates an essential place in the life of faith to the communal component. What this text will show is that Kierkegaard does allocate an essential place in the life of faith to language.

My examination of this text will not only show that Professor Taylor's charge against Kierkegaard is mistaken, it will also reveal a profound irony in his charge. Professor Taylor has confused Kierkegaard's understanding of the religious life of faith with Kierkegaard's understanding of the demonic life. In fact, it seems that what Professor Taylor takes Kierkegaard's conception of the life of faith to be is actually what Kierkegaard would call the demonic. The key again to perceiving this mistaken interpretation is the role, or lack thereof, that language plays in the life of faith and the demonic life.

In this text one not only sees that language is the decisive factor in distinguishing the life of faith from the demonic life, one also begins to recognize the relation that language has to freedom in Kierkegaard's thought. Freedom, of course, for Kierkegaard, lies at the very heart of the life of faith, just as unfreedom lies at the heart of the demonic life. I will suggest that this text clearly shows that language is decisive for the life of faith precisely because it is decisive for freedom's concrete actualization.

What is it that Taylor says about Kierkegaard? To Taylor's credit, he seems right on target in recognizing the importance of social or communal relations in the life of the faithful self.

Relations are ontologically definitive—to be is to be related. In terms of human being, selfhood is essentially social, spirit fundamentally intersubjective. Concrete individuality can arise *only* in community, with other free subjects. Apart from such interrelation, the self remains totally abstract, utterly indefinite, and completely incomprehensible.[2]

Taylor's main criticism of Kierkegaard is that he failed to recognize, and indeed explicitly denied, in his analysis of faith any essential role to such communal relations. Taylor does not want to deny the importance of the individual and so agrees with Kierkegaard to this extent, but he claims that *to be*, that is, to be a fully actualized concrete individual, *is to be related,* and that for Kierkegaard *to be*, that is, to be a fully actualized individual (and for Kierkegaard this is the same as living the life of faith) *is to be isolated* from other individuals. As Taylor puts it, life in community is for Kierkegaard a "concession to the human weakness of being unable to bear the isolation of spiritual individuality."[3] And further he claims that for Kierkegaard, "The birth of such spiritual individuality requires severing the umbilical cord of sociality through the difficult labor of differentiating self and other. The one who understands this spiritual pilgrimage ever remains a lonely wayfarer."[4]

Of course, Taylor recognizes that Kierkegaard is attacking "the crowd" when he speaks of society and agrees with Kierkegaard that the faithful self cannot exist in such thoughtless and mechanical associations. What Taylor thinks, however, is that Kierkegaard did not distinguish between a genuine community and "the crowd" and that, hence, when Kierkegaard rejects the latter he also rejects the former.

A major problem with Kierkegaard's argument at this point is his refusal to acknowledge the possibility of a form of human community that enhances and does not abolish responsible individuality. Certainly he is correct in criticizing the mode of human association in which individuals are differentiated neither from one

---

[2]*Journeys to Selfhood,* 274.

[3]Ibid., 180.

[4]Ibid.

another nor from their surroundings. To exist primarily as a reflex of the influences of others rather than as a self-conscious center of responsible decision is to fail to achieve the full potentiality of self-hood. But Kierkegaard errs in the opposite direction. While the mindless identification of the self with others cannot be accepted as the most complete realization of self, neither can a form of existence that puts primary emphasis on the self's life of isolated individuality to the exclusion of participation in genuine human community be accepted as the fulfillment of the self.[5]

In a key passage, Taylor summarizes his criticism of Kierkegaard and discloses the heart of its irony. The italicized passages indicate that what Taylor understands as the life of faith is actually closer to what Kierkegaard himself understands as the demonic life. Notice that the italicized points directly involve language and freedom, or more precisely their supposed absence, in the life of faith.

Since he [Kierkegaard] regards Christianity as the most complete realization of individual selfhood, and because he understands Christian faith to be an inwardness that cannot become outward, he argues that the fullest realization of selfhood is to be found in isolated individuality rather than in community with other selves. Since he sees faith as lying within the inwardness of the self, Kierkegaard must contend that at the deepest level, the level of one's faith, *persons cannot communicate with one another*. Each individual is *locked up* within the inwardness of his own subjectivity. Selves are discrete and isolated, and where the most profound issue of the self's life is concerned, there is no possibility of relating to other selves. This is the point of his repeated emphasis on *silence*.[6]

If I were to translate Taylor's English phrase *locked up* into Danish, I might use the word *Indesluttede*, which is the word that Kierkegaard uses (CA, 123) to define the demonic. Thomte has translated the Danish into the English phrase *inclosing reserve* (CA, 123), while Lowrie's earlier translation rendered *Indesluttede* as *shut-upness*.[7] One interesting feature of all of these phrases is that they

[5]*Kierkegaard's Pseudonymous Authorship*, 253-54.

[6]Ibid., 350.

[7]Søren Kierkegaard, *The Concept of Dread*, translated with an introduction and notes by Walter Lowrie (Princeton: Princeton University Press, 1957).

connote what one might call *caged-upness*, or, more to the point, they connote the absence of freedom.

Although I will follow Thomte's rendering of *Indesluttede* as *inclosing reserve*, there is a suggestive element in Lowrie's notion of *shut-upness*. The suggestion lies in *shut-upness*'s connotation of both a sense of unfreedom, in that if someone is shut-up he cannot do as he will, and a sense of *silence*, in that the phrase *shut-up!* is a colloquial command or request for silence. The point here is that *Indesluttede* is connected with *both unfreedom and silence*, and that Kierkegaard uses the term to characterize the demonic, while Taylor characterizes the life of faith in Kierkegaard as a life that is "locked up," in some sense unfree and silent.

In order to grasp the irony of Taylor's criticism of Kierkegaard, one must turn to a more detailed analysis of Kierkegaard's view of the demonic life. One will discover that Kierkegaard's dialectical discussion of the demonic also says a great deal about the life of faith. I hope, again, to show that for Kierkegaard language and freedom figure decisively in the life of faith, just as silence and unfreedom figure decisively in the demonic life.

Constantly a critic of the spiritlessness of his own time, Kierkegaard begins the section "Anxiety about the Good (the Demonic)" (CA, 118) by charging that his generation has either not reflected at all on the demonic or that its reflections have been superficial. Most reflections on the demonic get arrested on "one or another unnatural sin," in which there is an "ascendency of the bestial" over the human (CA, 118). The explanation given for this ascendency is usually in terms of what Kierkegaard calls "the bondage of sin," that is, the demonic life is claimed to be a manifestation of that bondage.

It is interesting that Kierkegaard characterizes the bondage of sin in terms of *language*, or, more precisely, *speech*, which is for Kierkegaard the most concrete form of expression. Kierkegaard likens the person who is in the bondage of sin to a game in which two people are concealed under a cloak, *appearing to be one person*. In this game, "one speaks and the other gesticulates arbitrarily without any relation to what is said" (CA, 119). The life in the bondage of sin, then, is a life abstracted from itself, a life *lacking reflexive integrity*. A decisive manifestation of such a bondage of sin is the disparity between what is said (an outward expression) and one's behavior (also an outward expression).

Like the bondage of sin, the demonic is also characterized by a *lack of reflexive integrity*. The difference, however, is that the lack of reflexive integrity in the demonic is more radical, for here the disparity is not just between two outward expressions, what one says and what one does, but between one's outward expressions, what one says and does, and one's inward state. Kierkegaard puts it this way: "The bondage of sin is an unfree relation to the evil, but the demonic is an unfree relation to the good" (CA, 119). In the bondage of sin, one's inward anxiety is about evil, and this anxiety gives expression to one's condemnation of evil, even though one finds one's behavior at odds with this expression. There is here something of an integrity between the inner and outer, but a lack of integrity between the outward expression and the outward behavior. In the demonic, one's inward anxiety is about the good, and this anxiety is reflected in a radical disparity between one's outward expressions, one's sayings and doings, and one's inward states.

For Kierkegaard, *the good* "signifies the restoration of freedom, redemption, salvation, or whatever one would call it" (CA, 119). For the purposes here then, I will say that for Kierkegaard the demonic who is anxious about the good is anxious about freedom, that freedom is the good. Just as freedom is the good, so is unfreedom evil. This is what the individual who is in the bondage of sin is anxious about; he is anxious about evil, unfreedom.

Freedom signifies an *integrity* of expression and behavior and of the outward and the inward. Merely choosing to do X, when one could have chosen Y, does not in itself constitute freedom. Indeed it would not be freedom if for some reason one does not or cannot actually fulfill one's choice. Freedom presupposes an integration of both option and fulfillment. If I say, "I choose to do X," but in fact I can't do X, or don't do it, then freedom is not concretely actualized, and I lack any integrity between my inward "choice" and its concrete fulfillment. Such a concretely actualized freedom and its correlated integrity of the inward and the outward just *is* for Kierkegaard, *the good*. The opposite of the good, which Kierkegaard sometimes calls evil and sometimes sin, is characterized by *unfreedom* and the kind of dis-integration found in the game where the two persons pose as one.

For Kierkegaard, then, the individual in the bondage of sin is anxious about evil, about sin, about unfreedom. Insofar as he is in the bondage of sin, he is *in unfreedom and anxious about unfreedom*. He knows that "No matter how deep an individual has sunk, he can still sink deeper, and this 'can' is the object of anxiety" (CA, 113). As unfree, the individual in the bondage of sin exists in dis-integration, and his anxiety is about a deeper unfreedom and a deeper dis-integration.

In contrast to the individual in the bondage of sin, the demonic individual is more radically evil; indeed, the former is good in comparison to the latter. The reason for this difference in character is that the individual in the bondage of sin is anxious about the proper enemy of faith, that is, unfreedom, sin. The demonic individual, on the other hand, is anxious about the good, about freedom. Being *in* sin, the demonic individual is unfree and dis-integrated but is anxious about and flees from the good, from freedom, from integrity.

The anxieties felt by the individual in the bondage of sin and by the demonic individual are both different from the anxiety felt in innocence. Anxiety about unfreedom and anxiety about freedom are both anxieties *in sin*, not the anxiety of innocence, which is the anxiety *before sin*. The innocent individual exists in unfreedom but of a different sort than that possible after freedom is existentially posited, that is, after it has become actual and concrete. In innocence, anxiety is produced when freedom appears before it in possibility. In the Fall, freedom is concretely actualized but paradoxically lost in the same act. Hence, after the Fall, when freedom is no longer a mere possibility but an actuality, its opposite, unfreedom, also actually exists. The individual *in sin* has lost his freedom and is unfree in this sense; the individual *in innocence* has never been free and is unfree in this sense.

Recognizing the different senses of unfreedom in the demonic life and in the innocent life will help one to see the difference in the objects of their anxieties. This distinction is important because on the surface the demonic individual and the innocent individual appear to be anxious over the *same thing*, namely the good, freedom.

Both then, seem to be different from the individual who is in the bondage of sin and is anxious about evil, unfreedom. The principle at work in Kierkegaard's analysis seems to be something like this: the innocent individual is anxious about the good, about a freedom he has never concretely actualized, whereas the demonic individual is anxious about the good, which is the freedom he has concretely actualized and lost at the same time.

The demonic individual knows something about the good, freedom, that the innocent individual is ignorant of: it can be lost. What he knows is that freedom is an equivocal good. While freedom may offer the extraordinary advantage of an integrated existence, its concrete actualization brings with it an awareness of responsibility, guilt, and death. Because freedom is ambiguous, because it can be lost, the demonic individual then is like someone who anxiously flees a love relation because he knows correctly how easily it can be broken. The demonic individual is anxious about the good.

According to Kierkegaard, the defining characteristic of the demonic life in which by some sinister logic it is the good about which the individual is anxious, is *inclosing reserve*. He says, "The demonic is unfreedom that wants to close itself off. . . . The demonic is *inclosing reserve and the unfreely disclosed.* . . . inclosing reserve is precisely the mute and when it is to express itself, this must take place contrary to its will . . . " (CA, 123). Notice again how language and freedom figure, albeit negatively, in this definition of the demonic. Since for Kierkegaard, "freedom is precisely the expansive" (CA, 123), inclosing reserve, which is evidently the opposite of the expansive, must be precisely unfreedom. Such an unfree inclosing reserve is also said to be "the mute." What Kierkegaard means by this phrase is the very heart of his argument.

What does Kierkegaard's definition of the demonic in terms of an *unfree silence* mean? One must be very careful at this point not to think that the "muteness" Kierkegaard speaks of is a literal silence. The demonic individual can and does use language; he does engage in expression. But such expression "takes place contrary to its will." The muteness, the silence of the demonic individual is a subtle and deceptive silence. It is a silence that "lies" behind the unfree expression. Here there is no reflexive integrity between one's inner will and one's outward expression.

For example, consider the aesthetic action in a stage play. The expression of a stage actor does not originate personally in his own freely chosen inward intention but with the externally imposed text of the play. When Richard Burton says *as Hamlet*, "To be or not to be," he is not literally silent, but he is subtly silent in that Richard Burton is saying nothing *as Richard Burton, as himself*. When a person speaks *as himself*, there is an *integrity* of expression (the outward) and meaning, the content of the expression, what is expressed, that which originates (inwardly) in a freely chosen intention of the speaker. When a person speaks *as himself*, he has achieved reflexive integrity and takes full responsibility for what he has said as *his own*. Such an expression is no longer a deception, no longer a lie, no longer merely play, it is now that through which one is implicated in responsibility, and it is profoundly serious. The demonic individual flees from such responsibility and seriousness and turns his expressions into playful lies that close off his inward self from the world, from others. And this characterization is true of anyone who imagines that his expressions in the world are externally imposed by his social role. Such a "speaker" is subtly mute and lacks reflexive integrity; he is abstracted from himself, the world, and others; he is outside of inwardness and freedom.

This discussion brings one to a consideration of the opposite of the demonic life, the life of faith. The two lives are, of course, for Kierkegaard deceptively close but subtly and radically different. For Kierkegaard, the life of faith is the life of freedom, or at least the life in which freedom is the *telos;* it is a life that strives after reflexive integrity; it is a life in which language, or more precisely, the spoken word, figures decisively and positively.

In Professor Taylor's above quotation, which concerns the life of faith, he says that for Kierkegaard the faithful self is "locked up" within himself and cannot communicate with others. This description now seems to be exactly what Kierkegaard means by the demonic life and is a stark contrast to what he says about the life of freedom and its relation to language. Indeed, Kierkegaard says, "Freedom is always communicating. . . . unfreedom becomes more and more inclosed and does not want communication" (CA, 124).

And further, "Inclosing reserve is precisely muteness. Language, the word, *is precisely what saves*, what saves the individual from the empty abstraction of inclosing reserve. . . . For language does indeed imply communication" (CA, 124; my emphasis).

What Professor Taylor seems to miss in Kierkegaard, what makes him misunderstand Kierkegaard as advocating a silent, solitary path towards an inward and isolated salvation, is his failure to recognize the important distinction that Kierkegaard makes between the silence of inclosing reserve (demonic silence) and the silence of what he calls "lofty" inclosing reserve (faithful silence) (CA, 126). One can make sense of this distinction, however, only by recognizing the essential relation that language bears to freedom.

The distinction I made earlier between the stage actor's expression, what I will now call an *aesthetic expression*, and a reflexively integral expression of a concrete individual who claims the expression as his own, what I will now call an *existential expression*, again becomes relevant. Consider first aesthetic expression of the demonic type and its relation to freedom. If one speaks aesthetically and demonically, the words issue out of unfreedom—they are imposed externally against one's will. As such, these words are not one's own; they do not express one. That one's expression is not integrally related to one's inward self *shows* that one is not free in relation to one's words. For Kierkegaard this is a decisive sign; what decisively shows that one is unfree is one's unfree relation to one's expression.

In existential expression, what shows decisively through is one's freedom, for such reflexive integrity presupposes that one's expressions are one's own, and that presupposes that one is absolutely free in relation to one's words. Such existential expression is to the life of faith what aesthetic expression is to the demonic life; in the former, one's words concretely actualize one's freedom, whereas in the latter, one's words abstract one from oneself imprisoning one in unfreedom.

The difference between the silence of inclosing reserve and the silence of "lofty" inclosing reserve is this issue of freedom. In demonic silence wherein the speaker does not speak as himself, what shows is that the speaker is unfree in relation to his words. In the life of faith there is also a place for silence, but it is a "lofty" place.

What this description means is that in faithful, existential expression the speaker is absolutely free in relation to his words, and hence *absolutely able to be silent*—and this is a literal and absolutely freely chosen silence. Here, lofty silence is not a sign of unfreedom, but just the opposite: it is as much a sign of the absolutely free relation the faithful self bears to his words as is his reflexively integral speech. Since his words are *his,* since he is free in relation to them, he is absolutely able to speak or to be silent. Integral speech *and* lofty silence both characterize decisively the faithful self.

Why does the demonic flee from freedom into the existential muteness of unfree expression? Kierkegaard's answer is that the demonic self lacks the faith to extricate himself from the anxieties generated by the recognition of freedom's equivocal and ambiguous nature. Because he is not able to overcome the anxieties attendant to (but transcended by faith) a life of freedom, he seeks at all cost to flee from integral expression, for it would bring with it the concrete actualization of what he can not bear, freedom.

One reason that the demonic individual flees from integral expression is that he recognizes that it, like the freedom it concretely actualizes, is equivocal. Even though language, if properly and freely appropriated, is the means of integration, even though it is "precisely what saves," it is liable to be misinterpreted, and moreover it makes one responsible for what one says, and it bares one's soul and makes one vulnerable to attack, scorn, and abuse. Like the ambiguities of freedom, the ambiguities of freedom's most decisive sign, reflexively integral speech, are too much for the demonic to bear.

The demonic individual is clever and insidious in his evasions of reflexive integrity. The clearest case of this is his "use" of language. For Kierkegaard, language is the perfect medium for freedom's concrete actualization.[8] Since the demonic may know this,

---

[8]*Either/Or,* vol. 1, especially in the section entitled "The Immediate States of the Erotic or the Musical Erotic," 45-134. Remembering that for Kierkegaard spirit = self and the self = that which relates itself to itself, and that such integral selfhood = freedom, one can see the intimate connection between language and freedom (spirit) in the following passages: "Not until the spiritual is posited is language vested with its rights. . . . As a medium, language is the one absolutely

but wants to evade freedom, he devises ways to "use" language to avoid precisely language's potential for integrity. Given that language is precisely what saves, and that its felicitous use can actualize freedom, one can see how insidious and how clever the demonic individual is when he uses precisely what saves to forward his demonic project of evading what saves.

Kierkegaard's discussion of "the sudden" sheds light on the demonic project of evasion. Kierkegaard claims that *"The demonic is the sudden.* . . . when the content is reflected upon, the demonic is defined as inclosing reserve; when time is reflected upon, it is defined as the sudden" (CA, 129). And further he says, "The sudden, like the demonic, is anxiety about the good. The good signifies continuity, for the first expression of salvation is continuity" (CA, 130).

Why does Kierkegaard associate the good with continuity? Why does he say that "the first expression of salvation is continuity"? His reason seems to be tied up with his idea that faithful existence is an existence concretely integrated into time. The faithful self accepts the fact that the past is over and done, that is, the past is present to the faithful self *as past;* and the faithful self courageously welcomes the future as the realm of the not-yet, the realm of possibilities that allow freedom to be concretely actualized, that is, the future is present to the faithful self *as future.* Such continuity in time is the very heart of an integrated faithful existence.

Kierkegaard clearly recognizes that language is the perfect medium for expressing temporal continuity, just as the sudden is the negation of continuity. He says,

> The words and the speaking, no matter how short when regarded *in abstracto,* always have a certain continuity for the reason that they

---

spiritually qualified medium" (65). "But that which religious enthusiasm wishes to have expressed is spirit, therefore it requires language" (71). In *Christian Discourses,* Kierkegaard makes it clear that the spiritual man, that is, the man who is authentically free, is implicated in an obligation to communicate. He says, "Thus the goods of the spirit are in and for themselves essentially communication . . . [CD, 122]. Then by instruction, by reproof, by encouragement, by comfort, he [the spiritual man] communicates these goods, directly making others rich" (CD, 125). Significantly, the central doctrine of Christianity for Kierkegaard is the Incarnation. This was a historical event in which God, Spirit, communicated itself to man through the revelation of the *Word* made flesh.

are heard in time. But the sudden is a complete abstraction from continuity, from the past and from the future. (CA, 132)

Because of the connection between language and continuity, an ideal representation of the sudden is found in the silence of aesthetic mime. If, for example, the demonic negation of the continuity is to be properly represented on the stage as Mephistopheles, words must be avoided altogether. The sudden is captured in the leap of Mephistopheles through the window, and in his silent stationary position in the attitude of the leap. A walk would suggest continuity. He must leap, and move with sudden, detached, and abrupt action.

Although the demonic negation of continuity in the sudden can be represented aesthetically through the abrupt and silent gestures of the mimic art of the stage actor, its most insidious and most clever manifestation is *the appearance of continuity* in an individual's daily life. Since, for Kierkegaard, language is the perfect medium for expressing continuity, whenever it is used there is at least the appearance of continuity. Yet this continuity is deceptive, for only in an *integral* use of language does *real* continuity exist. The demonic individual who is anxious about real continuity may avoid it through the insidious cleverness of the *contentless* and the *boring* (CA, 132). Such empty talk is "a continuity in nothingness," talk without substance, talk that conceals rather than reveals, dis-integrates rather than integrates, talk—incessant talk—that ironically characterizes a deeper silence. Here the demonic flees from faithful selfhood, from freedom, integrity, continuity, and all the rest by flirting with the very means through which these find concrete actualization, language itself. Such a perverted "use" of language may just be the height of demonic cleverness, but it is finally a tragico-comical attempt to conceal an infinite emptiness and a demonic anxiety about the good.

At point after point, Kierkegaard connects language (at least its felicitous use) to freedom, and then connects both to the integrated life of faith. And just as consistently, on the other hand, he connects silence (not the lofty type) and unfreedom to each other and to the demonic life. Assuming that language in its proper integral use presupposes a genuine community as opposed to "the crowd," one can thus conclude that Kierkegaard's insistence on the essential role that language has in the concrete actualization of freedom, and hence its essential role in the life of faith, shows that Professor Taylor and other like-minded critics of Kierkegaard are profoundly mistaken.

VIII

The Concept of Anxiety: The Keystone of the Kierkegaard-Heidegger Relationship

by Dan Magurshak

In the opinion of many, the relationship that exists between the thought of Søren Kierkegaard and that of Martin Heidegger hardly needs further investigation. They would say that the existential analysis of *Being and Time* owes much to Kierkegaard, and that Heidegger, in the three by now famous footnotes that he accords the Danish thinker in that work, generously acknowledges the debt. They would then add that in *Being and Time* Heidegger goes far beyond Kierkegaard's "existentiell" account of existence by exhibiting the fundamental "existential" structure of human existence. Finally, they would note that when Heidegger focuses his later thinking upon the truth of being and upon man's relation to it, he properly characterizes Kierkegaard, whose work is dominated by the Western metaphysical mode of thought, as having nothing whatever to say about being. For Heidegger, Kierkegaard is "not a thinker, but a religious writer . . . in accord with the destining belonging to his age."[1]

The matter, however, is not that simple. A close study of Kierkegaard's works, particularly *The Concept of Anxiety*, alongside Heidegger's writings, especially *Being and Time*, suggests a number of interesting theses. It suggests, first, that the footnotes mentioned above neither properly acknowledge the substantial debt that *Being and Time* owes to Kierkegaard nor accurately assess the latter's thought. Second, it suggests that while Heidegger's existential analysis is at times more fundamental than some of Kierkegaard's reflections, the latter's reflections, even in their Christian context, are often as fundamental and sometimes richer than Heidegger's. Finally, it suggests that any complete study of the relationship between the thinkers must acknowledge the multi-leveled complexity of that relationship.

At issue in this last thesis is the adequate interpretation of human existence and the contributions that each of these two very different approaches makes to this endeavor. This issue, in turn, raises questions about interpretation that demand answers. For example, are existential phenomenological investigations based upon a concern for being Christian commensurable with those arising from a quest for being? Can they be compared to and contrasted with one another on an equal footing or must the findings of one approach inevitably be subsumed as a subordinate, less profound portion of the other? As it stands, Heidegger describes Kierkegaard's project as "onto-theological" and decidedly "metaphysical," while Kierkegaard might have viewed Heidegger's quest as a more sophisticated version of "spiritless," "aesthetic" metaphysics. One also needs to ask whether some perspective permits one to view the projects of both thinkers critically and impartially for the sake of advancing beyond them.

To be sure, such questions can be adequately explored only when the entire projects of both Kierkegaard and Heidegger are studied. They are mentioned only to provide the framework for the

---

[1]Martin Heidegger, *The Question Concerning Technology*, trans. William Lovitt (New York: Harper and Row, 1977) 91.

theses of this present, limited effort by reminding both the author and the reader of the full scope and complexity of the task at hand. This essay confines itself to a study of the seminal influence that Kierkegaard's *The Concept of Anxiety* exercises upon the existential analysis of Heidegger's *Being and Time*. It first shows that Kierkegaard's insights into anxiety, freedom, temporality, the demonic, and disclosive existential certainty exert major formative influence upon Heidegger's analysis of *Dasein*. In so doing it will show that the latter's assessment of Kierkegaard's work is largely unsupportable, at least as it concerns *The Concept of Anxiety*. It then points out the difference between the analyses and the approaches of the two thinkers while still maintaining that their various insights into existence often correct and complement one another. Insights that Heidegger borrows from Kierkegaard are transformed to suit his own quest for being, sometimes for better, sometimes for worse, but in no way can one claim that Kierkegaard's analyses and approach have been totally and adequately subsumed by those of *Being and Time*. The analysis of existence pursued by each thinker can still contribute to the ongoing task of interpreting human existence. Finally, this essay will outline briefly three of the major areas that must be investigated if the relationship between the work of these thinkers is to be further clarified. Its own conclusions, of course, will be only provisional until this task is accomplished.

The Indebtedness

When one explores the relationship between Kierkgaard's thought and Heidegger's existential analysis in *Being and Time,* one must face squarely the radical difference between their projects. Kierkegaard reflects upon the existing individual as capable of genuine and complete existential integrity or wholeness only through a God-relationship based upon the belief in a divine redeemer. Heidegger, on the other hand, thinks about human being in its distinctive relation to the truth of being itself. Thus, he pursues his existential analysis only as far as is necessary to clarify the question about being. In spite of this difference, fundamental insights developed in *The Concept of Anxiety* permeate and fructify the partial existential analysis of *Being and Time*.

According to two footnotes in the latter work, Heidegger takes Kierkegaard's little book seriously. He remarks in one place that Kierkegaard is "The man who has gone farthest in analyzing the phenomenon of anxiety . . ."[2] He also notes that although one learns more from Kierkegaard's "edifying" writings than one does from his Hegelian-dominated "theoretical" ones, *The Concept of Anxiety* is an exception to this rule.[3] Heidegger learned a great deal from this particular theoretical work, and, in relation to his existential analysis, he might well have learned more.

Existence and Anxiety

In *The Concept of Anxiety*, as in his other pseudonymous works, Kierkegaard is concerned with existence as the task of complete self-realization or existential wholeness. He describes this self-realization as the positing and maintaining of the synthesis of the psychical and physical aspects of existence by spirit, that is, by the capacity for free self-determination (CA, 81, 90). To exist is to be constantly in the process of realizing or failing to realize this task; and if a person succeeds, he is truly himself, that is, lucidly aware of all aspects of his mental-physical-spiritual existence, and living as the free, responsible self-disclosure of all that he is. In such a life there is no repression or self-deception of any kind; a person lives in full, existential self-disclosure. For Kierkegaard, such complete self-realization occurs only as Christian existence. "[I]n relating itself to itself and in willing to be itself," says Kierkegaard, "the self rests [or has its ground] transparently in the power that established it," that is, God (CA, xvii).

But if existence is a lifelong task to be accomplished, how does a human being become aware of himself as this task? Kierkegaard says that anxiety as a fundamental mode of affective self-awareness "is the pivot upon which everything turns" (CA, 43). Because

---

[2]Martin Heidegger, *Being and Time,* trans. John Macquarrie and Edward Robinson (New York: Harper and Row, 1962) H. 190, n. iv.

[3]*Being and Time,* H. 235, n. vi.

a human being is a synthesis to be accomplished, "he can be in anxiety." In fact, "to learn what it is to be in anxiety . . . is an adventure that every human being must go through. . . . Whoever has learned to be anxious in the right way has learned the ultimate" (CA, 155). The experience of anxiety is the sine qua non for existential development. It is not surprising, then, that Kierkegaard's analysis of the concept of anxiety contains at least in schematic form a phenomenological description of many essential aspects of existence. To be sure, the intent of *The Concept of Anxiety* is not to provide an explicit existential analysis in Heidegger's sense. It is a "simple" rather than speculative, "psychologically orienting," ontic "deliberation on the dogmatic issue of hereditary sin." Thus, Kierkegaard conducts his investigation in the context of the Christian concern for hereditary sin and the revealed possibility of salvation. Nonetheless, when one turns to *Being and Time*, one finds existential analyses, now secularized, exactly parallel to those of *The Concept of Anxiety*.

Throughout his philosophical life, Heidegger was concerned with the question of being and of man's relation to being's disclosure and concealment. In *Being and Time*, he attempts to raise anew the question of the sense of being in general and to answer it. But to raise the question properly, he finds it necessary to investigate the being of the entity that, in its very being, relates to being in general. This entity is *Dasein*, a term that describes man as the clearing of or the openness to being. It is the entity whose own being, articulated as care, is grounded in temporality. The existential analysis of *Dasein*—which in no way intends to provide a complete basis for a philosophical anthropology—is undertaken only to clarify the question about being itself. Intending to exhibit man's fundamental existential possibilities as modes of temporalizing, Heidegger then hopes to exhibit temporality as the horizon of the question about the sense of being in general. His overriding concern for being, however, does not prevent him from adopting an unmistakably Kierkegaardian approach to *Dasein*'s existence.

Heidegger calls *Dasein*'s being existence and describes it as something that one "has to be." It is a task, a burden that must be accomplished insofar as *Dasein* is the entity "whose being is at issue in its very being."[4] *Dasein* exists as a potential to be one's self that is either realized or passed by; one can either evade oneself in self-deceptive preoccupation with mundane, everyday busywork or live authentically as a finite, mortal, free being-in-the-world. As in Kierkegaard's approach, the issue in an important sense is existential wholeness, that is, living in a manner that lucidly appropriates oneself as a thrown, mortal, finite, yet self-determinative entity who lives with others among things. Heidegger, of course, does not use the Hegelian-sounding terminology of "synthesis" that one finds in Kierkegaard's work; nonetheless, the existential wholeness brought about by resoluteness seems to be the same integrity that concerns Kierkegaard. To exist as a thrown, mortal potential for self-determination is to exist as what Kierkegaard calls the psychic-physical (thrown) entity whose synthesis (wholeness) is posited and maintained by spirit (one's capacity for self-determination). It is to live as complete self-disclosure. Like Kierkegaard, Heidegger also asserts that the possibility of such wholeness is first disclosed to a human being through the fundamental mode of affective self-discovery that he, too, calls anxiety. Here, as in *The Concept of Anxiety*, anxiety is necessary for the accomplishment of existence.

How and why both thinkers describe this anxiety as essential to complete existential integrity shows another major Kierkegaardian influence upon *Being and Time*. To be sure, Kierkegaard's analysis, unlike Heidegger's analysis of anxiety, distinguishes among various forms of anxiety that correspond to various phases of existential self-development; thus, *The Concept of Anxiety* explicitly recognizes the "developmental" history of the individual, a history simply not discussed in *Being and Time*. However, all forms of anxiety manifest certain essential features in their nature and function.

According to *The Concept of Anxiety*, anxiety in all of its forms is an anxiety about one's own potential for existence; it concerns one's "being able" as one's capacity for self-determination. A person is anxious either about "freedom's actuality as the possibility of pos-

---

[4]Ibid., H. 11-13.

sibility" or about some possibility that is open to his choice (CA, 49, 42). A person is thus anxious about "nothing," "nothing" as understood as the nonactual, the possible whose actualization lies in the future (CA, 41). But this possibility does not belong to the external world; it is always one's own. As Kierkegaard says, "anxiety is the dizziness of freedom which emerges when the spirit [freedom, the capacity for self-determination] wants to posit the synthesis and freedom looks down into its own possibility" (CA, 61). But simply because it concerns one's own potential freedom, it does not follow that one is at home with what anxiety discloses. Anxiety is in all cases "a sympathetic and an antipathetic sympathy" (CA, 42). An anxious person is both repelled and attracted to his capacity for self-determination. On the one hand, spirit is a friendly power because it enables the wholeness that it is one's task to accomplish; on the other hand, "it is in a sense a hostile power, for it constantly disturbs the relation between soul and body, a relation that indeed has persistence and yet does not have endurance inasmuch as it first receives the latter by the spirit" (CA, 43-44). No matter how far one has developed, unless one has achieved complete self-realization, anxiety's disclosure of possibility will always be disquieting. The possibility is that calls for decision will always be experienced as threatening the self-integration achieved thus far. Anxiety, then, in its essential moments, is the fundamental mode of affective self-awareness in which a person discovers the possibility of his free self-determination and its existential possibilities.

But even if a person becomes anxious, there is no guarantee that he will move forward. According to Kierkegaard, he may be liberated by choosing appropriately, that is, by making the qualitative leap of faith, or he may succumb. If he succumbs, he commits suicide in despair; if he is liberated, he is liberated through faith. According to Kierkegaard, "Anxiety is freedom's possibility, and only such anxiety is through faith absolutely educative because it consumes all finite ends and discovers all their deceptiveness" (CA, 156). This education occurs because "in possibility all things are equally possible and whoever has truly been brought up by possibility has grasped the terrible as well as the joyful. . . . He knows . . . that he can demand nothing of life, and that the terrible, perdition, and annihilation live next door to every man" (CA, 156). Because of this disclosure, anxiety enters a person, "searches out everything and anxiously torments everything finite and petty out of him, and then it leads him where he wants to go" (CA, 159). Kierkegaard is suggesting that when a person confronts his possibilities, especially those that pertain to his mortality and vulnerability, he separates finite, petty possibilities from those that are truly his own. In the anxious confrontation with his possibility, he sinks "absolutely," but then he may emerge in faith "from the depth of the abyss lighter than all the troublesome and terrible things in life" (CA, 158).

Turning to *Being and Time*, one finds that Heidegger has appropriated all of these structures in his first delineation of anxiety as one of *Dasein's* "fundamental modes of finding oneself."[5] According to Heidegger's analysis, anxiety is a fundamental mode of affective self-discovery that discloses care as the unifying structure of *Dasein's* being. When *Dasein* experiences anxiety, it is anxious in the face of its thrown being-in-the-world and, as Kierkegaard said, about its potentiality for being. From the perspective of daily, run-of-the-mill living, it is anxious about "nothing"; that is, it is uneasy about no particular entity nor specific project locatable in the "world" of its total network of involvements.[6] On the contrary, when *Dasein* is anxious, this network is experienced as insignificant. The "nothing" about which it is anxious is its own "being-possible," precisely what it is anxious about in *The Concept of Anxiety*. More specifically, *Dasein* confronts itself as "Being-*towards* one's most proper potentiality for being, that is, *being free for* the freedom of choosing and grasping oneself. Anxiety brings dasein before its *being free for* . . . the authenticity of his being as the possibility which it always already is."[7] Anxiety is thus a distinctive mode of affective self-discovery because it draws *Dasein* back out of fallen everydayness by disclosing to it authenticity and inauth-

---

[5]Ibid., H. 184-91.

[6]Ibid., H. 186-87. Here Heidegger alludes to exactly the same linguistic fact that Kierkegaard mentions to link the notion of anxiety with that of nothing.

[7]Ibid., H. 188.

enticity as possibilities of its being. Taking these terms, *authentic* and *inauthentic*, in the literal sense of "proper to one's own being," one sees that in *Being and Time*, as well as in *The Concept of Anxiety*, anxiety discloses to a person the possibility for existing as a full actualization of his potential, existential freedom. According to Heidegger, when *Dasein* experiences anxious self-disclosure, it feels "uncanny," "ill-at-ease," or "not-at-home." It feels threatened because the self-evident, familiar, complacent "being-at-home" in routine living is called into question by the disclosed capacity for responsible self-determination. The affective self-awareness of this possibility is uneasiness, because *Dasein* now realizes that simply drifting along in engagements into which one has fallen is not an appropriate expression of its "being-able." Most of the time, however, a person flees this uneasiness and loses himself in the tranquilizing bustle of ordinary life. A certain existential repression of his most fundamental capacity is thereby effected.

Thus far, it is apparent that what anxiety discloses according to *Being and Time* is precisely what it discloses according to *The Concept of Anxiety*, that is, one's capacity for self-determination. At this point, however, Heidegger apparently departs significantly from Kierkegaard's approach. The flight from oneself that is everyday life is more than a flight from one's capacity for responsible self-determination. When a person experiences himself as a thrown potentiality-for-being, he finds himself not only as possibly self-determinative, but also as possibly and inevitably *dead*, that is, mortal. As Heidegger puts it, "Anxiety is the self-discovery which is capable of maintaining the disclosure of the constant and utter threat to oneself which arises from one's most proper individualized being."[8] When a person is anxious, he confronts not only his possibility of authenticity but also "the nothing of the possible impossibility of [his] existence."[9] It is anxiety that affectively discloses death as a person's most proper, individualizing, insurpassable, certain, and yet temporally indefinite possibility.

---

[8]Ibid., H. 265-66.

[9]Ibid., H. 266.

Heidegger combines the two elements of anxious self-discovery when he discusses the phenomenon of what he terms the "existential conscience," the concrete attestation of *Dasein*'s possibility for existing in existential wholeness. According to Heidegger's analysis of conscience,[10] the call of conscience comes from oneself as the call of care. The caller is *Dasein* in its "uncanniness," in its primordial, thrown being-in-the-world as not-at-home, "the naked 'that' in the nothing of the world."[11] A person experiences this call as a summons from his own being that addresses him in his everyday living and summons him back to confront his "potentiality-for-becoming-burdened" (*schuldig*) in a lucid manner. This self-disclosure also shows that the potential for responsible self-determination is permeated with negativity. Heidegger here introduces a complex sense of "nothing" that one does not find in *The Concept of Anxiety*. The "nothing" that is disclosed is far more than the nothing of possibility. Through the call of conscience, a person discovers that he has been thrust into existence and abandoned to it; he is "not," therefore, the ground of his own being. In accomplishing this existence through the choice of projects, he pursues certain ones by "not" pursuing other possibilities, and as long as he lives, he may always fall back into concerns that do "not" truly express himself. Finally, one's thrown potential for self-determination is constantly threatened by its inevitable end, by death as the possibility of "not" being-in-the-world any longer. Conscience not only discloses this "nothingness" of existence, this multi-faceted finitude with which *Dasein* is burdened, it also demands that a person lucidly appropriate this burden by determining his life in light of it. It demands that a person realize himself as the mortal, free, finite disclosure of being by living authentically, that is, by living with an abiding lucid awareness of himself as finite freedom, an awareness that enables him to live in a manner most proper to himself as the concretely existing individual that he is. Since such disclosure occurs from the uneasiness of anxiety; anxiety is for Heidegger, as it is for Kierkegaard, a necessary condition for complete self-realization.

---

[10]Ibid., H. 271-88.

[11]Ibid., H. 276-77.

Recall that for Kierkegaard, anxiety saves through faith by educating through possibility. Somehow, a sinking into the abyss of possibility, especially that of perdition and annihilation, makes possible an emergence in complete self-realization. In such confrontation with the possible, Heidegger also discovers the possibility of "salvation," but here the education occurs not through faith, but through the lucid sense of one's own finitude. As Kierkegaard's individual sinks into the abyss only to be able to make the leap of faith, Heidegger's *Dasein* is overwhelmed by its thrown, limited, mortal freedom in order to become resolute. As the anxious individual finds all finite and petty ends crumbling around him, so does *Dasein*, "passing under the eyes of death," experience the scattering of all accidental and provisional possibilities in favor of its most proper involvement in the world.[12] If one but substitutes "everyday living" for Kierkegaard's "finite, petty" concerns, one can see an exact analogue between the function of educative anxiety in *The Concept of Anxiety* and the function of the anxious anticipation of death in *Being and Time*. Of course, without the notion of faith, Heidegger finds existential "salvation" only in the appropriation of man's multi-faceted finitude, a mode of life that Kierkegaard would consider just another form of despair. Nonetheless, the dynamic used by Heidegger is certainly Kierkegaardian.

One cannot deny that important differences exist between these two elaborate analyses of the nature and function of anxiety, and the questions that such differences raise will be discussed below. They do not, however, diminish the clear, substantial debt that *Being and Time* owes to *The Concept of Anxiety* in the matters already considered. Furthermore, the seminal influence of the former upon the latter does not stop here.

As anyone familiar with the work already knows, *The Concept of Anxiety* is more than a phenomenological analysis of the various forms of anxiety. It contains, sometimes explicitly but often implicitly, an ontology of the basic structures and developmental phases of human being. It includes exploratory analysis of lived

---

[12]Ibid., H. 382.

time, of the "demonic" evasion of one's potential freedom, and of existential truth as disclosure, all of which find their way into *Being and Time* in some form or other. Since the relationship between the "demonic," that is, "anxiety about the good," and existential truth parallels the relationship between Heidegger's inauthentic and authentic existence, they will be considered together. First, however, a brief examination of Kierkegaard's reflections on time and of their apparent influence on *Being and Time* is in order.

Existential Temporality

In one of his notes that refer to Kierkegaard, Heidegger assesses the former's treatment of time. "He clings to the ordinary conception of time, and defines the 'moment of vision' with the help of 'now' and 'eternity.' When Kierkegaard speaks of 'temporality,' what he has in mind is man's 'being-in-time.' Time as within-time-ness knows only the 'now'; it never knows a moment of vision. If, however, such a moment gets experienced in an existentiell manner, then a more primordial temporality has been presupposed."[13] Admittedly, Kierkegaard's analysis is often obscure, and it does not discuss temporality as the sense or ground of man's being; nonetheless, a careful reading shows that it can hardly be classified as a variation on the "ordinary conception of time" or as simply concerned with man's "within-time-ness." On the contrary, it foreshadows some of the most significant aspects of Heidegger's own notion of temporality.

In chapter 3 of *The Concept of Anxiety*, Kierkegaard simply states that "anxiety is the moment" (CA, 81). The discussion then considers the traditional philosophical notions of time and the moment and judges them inadequate for grasping the historical time of existence. As Heidegger later does in *Being and Time*, Kierkegaard shows that the ordinary notion of time, properly described as an infinite succession, an infinite vanishing, is replete with conceptual problems and actually lacking in the significant divisions of past time, present time, and future time. It therefore has no present, and if it speaks of the moment at all, it knows it represen-

---

[13]Ibid., H. 338, n. iii.

tationally only as a *discrimen*, a boundary between one instant and the next, a boundary that is really nothing at all. He then investigates the temporal as it relates to man, "a synthesis of psyche and body" who is also "a synthesis of the temporal and the eternal" (CA, 85-89). By doing so, he strongly suggests an intrinsic relationship between temporality and man's being as a task of self-realization. This insight prefigures Heidegger's claim that temporality grounds human being. But how are anxiety, time, and the moment related?

Kierkegaard describes the moment as a "figurative expression" (CA, 87); both the Danish and German words mean literally "a blink of the eye." He then explicates the moment as a designation "of time in the fateful conflict when it is touched by eternity," "the first reflection of eternity in time" (CA, 87, 88). "Time" in this context seems to mean the ordinary time of "passing by," and eternity, whatever else it means for Kierkegaard as a Christian, is clearly identified with spirit, with freedom as the capacity for synthesis, for self-determinative existence that gives existence the endurance of commitment rather than mere persistence in time.

When one is committed to a task, for instance, to marriage or to becoming Christian, one is engaged in an enduring commitment characterized by growth and deepening. Time does not then simply pass; one uses it to one's advantage and in such "use" the designations of past, present, and future become significant as phases of development. Since it is anxiety that discloses freedom's, spirit's, or the eternal's possibility, the experience of anxiety is the moment, "that ambiguity in which time [as passing by] and eternity [as freedom's possibility for enduring] touch each other, and with this the concept of *temporality* is posited, whereby time constantly intersects eternity and eternity constantly pervades time" (CA, 89). Kierkegaard also points out that "only with the moment does history begin" because only with the positing of temporality do the aforementioned temporal distinctions arise. In anxiety a person realizes, often prereflectively and predeliberatively, that he has potential, that he has a future to be freely determined. At the same moment, he discovers, in light of this future, what he has been and the repeatability of this having-been. He thus stands at the crossroads of a decision, where his personal history as growing endurance in commitment or as continuing evasion of such commitment begins. He now exists as truly temporal and not merely as a natural psycho-physical organism persisting in time.

In all of this, Kierkegaard notes that the future has priority; "the future in a certain sense signifies more than the present and the past because in a certain sense the future is the whole of which the past is a part, and the future can in a certain sense signify the whole." A person is genuinely temporal when he lives toward the future, and in doing so, he achieves existential integrity. In light of the future, he appropriates his past in a meaningful way in living the present. As Kierkegaard says, "The moment and the future in turn posit the past," and the Christian concept for this existential temporal unity is the "fullness of time." In it, one describes "the moment as the eternal, and yet this eternal is also the future and the past" (CA, 89, 90). Anxiety, then, since it is about possibility, is about the future because "the possible corresponds exactly to the future. For freedom, the possible is the future and the future is for time the possible" (CA, 91).

Much of this Kierkegaardian analysis is mirrored in Heidegger's own attempt in *Being and Time* to ground the being of *Dasein* in temporality. For him, both authentic and inauthentic existence are modes of temporalizing. Anxiety, however, enables authentic temporalizing because it discloses a person to himself as thrown into existence at a given historical time complete with a definite cultural and historical heritage.[14] His existence includes the past of his community, and anxiety (in disclosing a person's throwness) discloses certain aspects of both his collective and personal past as possibly repeatable, that is, as possibilities. (Kierkegaard also notes that if it can be said at all that one is anxious about the past, one can be anxious only about its possible repetition [CA, 89].) In anxiety, a person, aware of his future but inevitable death, comes back to these repeatable possibilities and in light of his mortality may choose to realize the possibilities most proper to himself. Since anxiety is the disclosure of a person's thrown potential for being-in-the-world, it enables an authentic existence in which the future

---

[14]Ibid., H. 342-44.

is primary. It is in light of the future that one returns to one's past, and, in a moment of vision, chooses to actualize the proper possibilities in the present.[15] For Heidegger as well as for Kierkegaard, the moment makes the past significant in light of the future, and therein lies existential wholeness. The Kierkegaardian notions of existential time, an integrity grounded in time, the priority of the future, the moment of decision, and existential repetition are alive and well in the analyses of *Being and Time*.

It appears, then, that Heidegger's assessment of Kierkegaard's account of time is hardly well founded. Like Heidegger, Kierkegaard clearly distinguishes the ordinary notion of time from his own exploratory notion of existential temporality. Nearly eighty years before *Being and Time*, Kierkegaard grapples with human being as temporal and with existential wholeness as somehow grounded in a future-oriented temporalization that gives significance to the past. Once again, anxiety is for both thinkers that which places one at the moment of decision about how one should live, about how time itself is experienced. To be sure, one also finds differences between the thinkers, particularly regarding the role that death as the limit of the future plays in existence, but this is discussed later. For now it is sufficient to note not only that Heidegger's assessment of Kierkegaard's notion of temporality is inaccurate, but also that this notion contains many essential features of Heidegger's own analysis of temporality.

Self-evasion and Existential Disclosure

Some of the more famous portions of *Being and Time*'s existential analysis focus upon two topics: first, the nature of everyday, fallen existence, an existence dominated by a public interpretation of existence, and second, the notion of *Dasein* as the self-disclosive disclosure of the various modes of being. The analysis of everydayness and the insight into *Dasein* as the openness, clearing, or disclosure of being have indeed become Heideggerian hallmarks. Nonetheless, if one carefully studies Kierkegaard's analysis of the "demonic," that is, of the "anxiety about the good," one again sees

---

[15]Ibid., H. 385.

that Heidegger owes a substantial debt to *The Concept of Anxiety* for important insights into both of these phenomena.

According to Kierkegaard, a person usually "sins" in the course of his development; that is, he lives in such a way that his psychical, bodily, and spiritual aspects are not properly integrated in a life of faith. Rather than living responsibly, he flees from the possibility of self-determination and anxiously suppresses it one way or another. He thereby chooses an unfree way of life characterized by anxiety about the good; in this case "good" signifies "the restoration of freedom, redemption, salvation, or whatever one would call it" (CA, 119). At this stage of existence, "freedom's possibility is anxiety" once again, at a more developed level. From the perspective of ongoing unfree existence, a person perceives this possibility of freedom precisely as the possibility of "unfreedom"; he does so because it threatens the ease and familiarity of the persisting disrelationship. Unlike other forms of anxiety, this form indicates a choice, one that might be called a "perverse" commitment to living in "unfreedom" by evading and repressing one's capacity for complete self-realization. Kierkegaard calls such existence "demonic" because it is anxiety about the good. It perceives the good as threatening.

Described in terms of self-disclosure, such anxiety is "inclosing reserve." It wants to close itself off and has freely chosen to "close itself up within itself." This "unfreedom makes itself a prisoner"; that is, "unfreedom becomes more and more inclosed and does not want communication." When an individual lives in this manner, he flees and represses any sense of his own capacity for freedom along with the choice that he has made to flee. He tries to close himself off completely from possible freedom; still, complete closure is impossible. As soon as he comes into contact in any way with this possibility, the latent anxiety about it becomes explicit. Such a life, then, is distinguished not only by *"inclosing reserve"* but also by *"the unfreely disclosed."* When confronted with appropriate cues, such a person involuntarily discloses, in ways familiar to any therapist, that he is anxious about the repressed possibility for self-determination (CA, 123-24).

Anxiety about the good, then, is at least in part anxiety about lucid self-awareness. As Kierkegaard says, "What determines whether the phenomenon is demonic is the individual's attitude toward disclosure, whether he will interpenetrate that fact [about himself] with freedom and accept it in freedom" (CA, 128-29). The most fundamental type of such anxiety would concern the possibility of self-determination itself, but one can experience such anxiety if there is any aspect of self—a mode of behavior, a psychological or physiological characteristic—that one refuses to acknowledge and appropriate as one's own. Here "there is something that freedom is unwilling to pervade" (CA, 130-31). One is therefore anxious about some aspect of disclosure or self-transparency, that is, about what Kierkegaard calls "the first expression of salvation," for lucid self-awareness is the first step in the free appropriation of one's own existence.

Because a demonic existence is self-evasive and repressive, it lacks existential integrity and continuity. The repressed fact about oneself, when it is involuntarily disclosed, appears as the "sudden," that which has no connection to the network of meanings of one's existence. Kierkegaard also describes such existence as "the contentless, the boring." Measured in terms of the growth and expansive self-development of freely chosen commitments, nothing is happening in demonic existence. There is, at best, "a continuity in nothingness," a stagnant passing of the time of one's life that results from a self-induced loss of freedom (CA, 130, 132-33).

If one now examines Heidegger's analysis of everyday existence and its relation to anxiety, one sees that this analysis seems to be rooted in Kierkegaard's analysis of anxiety about the good. According to *Being and Time*, *Dasein*'s absorption in the world manifests "something like a *fleeing* of dasein in face of itself."[16] But *Dasein* can flee only that which has been disclosed to itself about itself. Thus, "the turning away of falling is grounded . . . in anxiety."[17] It is a flight in face of the uncanniness felt in the presence of one's thrown, potential freedom. As in the case of anxiety about the good, a choice has already been made. One chooses unfreedom over freedom and simultaneously closes oneself up against one's

---

[16]Ibid., H. 185.

[17]Ibid., H. 186.

own potential freedom. One might therefore say that such a person "demonically" shuns lucid self-disclosure.

At the same time, Heidegger recognizes, as did Kierkegaard, that one cannot totally escape anxiety. Even as one flees, "the uncanniness pursues dasein constantly" as an implicit threat to everydayness. One is always latently anxious and one can at any time experience the disclosure of one's threatening potentiality for freedom. For Heidegger, everydayness is a constant repression of the most proper potential for existence, a repression always threatened by latent anxiety and therefore obliquely aware of what one wants to avoid at all costs. This self-evasion manifests itself in the modes of everyday disclosure—idle talk, curiosity, ambiguity— where no thing and no one, least of all oneself, is allowed to show itself as it is. [18] In such self-evasion, a person lives in anxiety about freedom's possibility, dreading the disclosure that is the first step to "salvation." And just as the demonic life deprives man of continuity and genuine self-development in Kierkegaard's view, so does self-evasive, inauthentic existence deprive him of what Heidegger calls the "self-constancy" of resoluteness. [19] As a flight from oneself, Heidegger's everydayness is exactly parallel to anxiety about the good. To state it exactly, the flight from the genuine self-disclosive experience of anxiety could be described as "anxiety about anxiety," a notion that fittingly names the phenomenon underlying both of these accounts.

As one can see from the above, an important feature of both everydayness and anxiety about the good is the disclosive nature of human being. In *The Concept of Anxiety*, Kierkegaard says that concrete existence is essentially a matter of "truth" where the latter is understood as disclosive, self-awareness. For example, in speaking of the demonic, Kierkegaard says that "inclosing reserve

---

[18]Ibid., H. 168-80. Even Kierkegaard's description of the intellectual form of the demonic foreshadows what Heidegger says of fallen existence: "the demonic is able to express itself as indolence that postpones thinking, as curiosity that never becomes more than curiosity, as dishonest self-deception, as effeminate weakness that constantly relies on others, as superior negligence, as stupid business, etc." (CA, 138).

[19]*Being and Time*, H. 322.

eo ipso signifies . . . untruth. But untruth is precisely unfreedom, which is anxious about disclosure" (CA, 128). In its anxiety about self-disclosure, the demonic is not honest about itself. It fails to acknowledge its potential for self-determination and, on the basis of this self-concealment, lives unfreely, untruthfully, because it does not manifest its repressed potentiality in its living. For Kierkegaard, "the content of freedom is truth, and truth makes man free. For this reason, truth [as self-disclosure] is the work of freedom," that is, "freedom [as lucid self-determination] constantly brings forth truth" (CA, 138).

To be sure, truth as a quality of a proposition is hardly at issue here. The truth that is the work of freedom, that is brought forth by it, is the true, honest life of a person who freely develops as a self-determining individual. In this development, his existence manifests the truth about human being. As Kierkegaard says, "truth is for the particular individual only as he himself produces it in action," that is, only as he embodies it in his life. "[T]he question is whether a person will in the deepest sense acknowledge the truth, will allow it to permeate his whole being, will accept all its consequences" (CA 138). In such existence one lives as the free, complete disclosure of existential truth. To be is to exist as the truth of human being in the sense that one's life embodies that truth. Thus, one refers to the "true Christian," the "true Nazi," or the "true Democrat" because they live out, as well as intellectually espouse, the principles that constitute such a life.

According to Kierkegaard, to exist as the truth is to exist in "inwardness and certitude," to be in "earnestness" about oneself as the task of developing one's personality as a unity of feeling and self-consciousness. In earnestness, one strives to exist as an affective, self-conscious, actual personality. Such earnestness is "the acquired originality of disposition, its originality preserved in the responsibility of freedom" (CA, 148). Disposition is the unity of feeling and self-consciousness wherein "the content of self-consciousness is felt by the subject as his own"; it acquires originality through the free appropriative synthesis of the elements of one's existence in a commitment that gives life a sense of continuity, an existential integrity enduring and deepening in time. In such in-

ward appropriation, one is "certain" of oneself; in such inwardness one realizes oneself as enduring existence (CA, 151).

In *Being and Time*, truth as disclosure is certainly conceived of
more comprehensively but, where it concerns *Dasein* itself, it is unmistakably Kierkegaardian. *Dasein* is the disclosure of its own
being, the being of other entities, and of being in general. Such disclosure "pertains equiprimordially to the world, being-in, and to
the self" but only "with dasein's disclosedness is the *most primordial* phenomenon of truth attained," that is, the truth understood
as a "being-uncovering."[20] Thus, "the most primordial, and indeed the most authentic, disclosedness in which dasein, as a potentiality-for-being can be, is the truth of existence," the disclosive
existence that Heidegger calls resoluteness.[21]

For both thinkers, then, truth is primarily a matter of how one
lives, and like Kierkegaard, Heidegger characterizes genuine,
honest—what he calls authentic—existence as grounded in the self-
disclosure accomplished by freely choosing one's commitments in
light of the basic components of existence. Heidegger also realizes
with Kierkegaard that existential truth is not merely an intellectual
truth. As Heidegger puts it, "To any truth there belongs a corresponding holding-for-true. The explicit appropriating of what has
been disclosed or discovered is *being*-certain. The primordial truth
of existence demands an equiprimordial *being*-certain."[22] One must
no only "understand" existence in such a way that one can write
about it; one must exist in the truth and endure in it as it "permeates" one's whole being. One must, to put it simply, live the
truth and maintain the complete disclosure of existence throughout life. It is this sort of life that anxiety makes possible.

It seems, then, that *The Concept of Anxiety* can be read as insem-
inating not only Heidegger's analysis of anxiety itself, but also his
notions of authentic temporality, of everyday, self-evasive lost-
ness in the "they," and of existence as truth. Heidegger himself is
willing to acknowledge this debt in a general fashion. In one of the

---

[20]Ibid., H. 220.

[21]Ibid., H. 221.

[22]Ibid., H. 307.

three notes on Kierkegaard in *Being and Time,* he states that "Søren Kierkegaard explicitly seized upon the problem of existence as an existentiell problem, and thought it through in a penetrating fashion." But for Heidegger, this analysis did not constitute an existential analysis because it was concerned with becoming and being a Christian in nineteenth-century Denmark. Furthermore, "the existential problematic was so alien to him [Kierkegaard] that, as regards his ontology, he remained completely dominated by Hegel and by ancient philosophy as Hegel saw it."[23] However, in light of the above comparison, this criticism seems unfounded. In spite of his use of Hegelian terminology such as "synthesis," "immediate," and so forth, Kierkegaard is as clearly struggling with the philosophical tradition as he is rethinking notions like anxiety, temporality, freedom, and truth from a more original perspective on existence. Even from the context of Christian concerns, a context Heidegger later calls "metaphysical," these innovative struggles of thought are powerful enough to illuminate Heidegger's own path of existential analysis. If Kierkegaard had, in fact, labored so completely under Hegel's domination, it is unclear how this thought could have so influenced *Being and Time.* Of course, radical differences do exist between the projects of the two thinkers, not only in the nature of their overall aims, but even in the analyses already discussed. Thus, the preceding effort is but a first step in the explication of their complex relationship and in the assessment of each as a contribution to the ongoing attempt to interpret human being.

Some Differences

In spite of the large debt Heidegger's existential analytic owes to *The Concept of Anxiety,* it is difficult to escape the sense that Heidegger's analytic, situated as it is in the context of the question of being, is more profound than Kierkegaard's approach to existence. In *Being and Time* being in general is at issue; the being of man, of things, of gods, and of all else that is must be radically

---

[23]See note 3 above.

questioned anew in a deconstruction of traditional ontology. In addition, the existential analysis of *Being and Time* discusses dimensions of existence that Kierkegaard does not discuss. Man is approached as the entity who (in his everyday being-in-the-world) understands being. As a disclosure not only of himself but of being in all its aspects, man is analyzed as care, the thrown, projective engagement in the world permeated with negativity and guaranteed of its no-longer-being-in-the-world. Care, in turn, is grounded in and unified by a temporality that is not merely a second synthesis expressive of the soul-body-spirit synthesis, but rather the fundamental synthesizing itself. *Dasein*'s possible modes of being, authenticity and inauthenticity, are modes of temporalizing that *Dasein* chooses to realize in life. As temporal, *Dasein* is also historical; and to be authentic is immediately to be part of the life of a historical community from which one selects possibilities. In all of this, of course, there is no discussion of the "eternal" in man. For Heidegger, phenomenological investigation does not uncover such a phenomenon; it is, rather, a result of the leap of faith that faith reads into a thoroughly finite existence. Thus, it is *Dasein*'s most finite possibility rather than its alleged "infinitude" that can educate it toward what "salvation" there is for it.[24]

Recall that Heidegger somehow intends this discussion to clarify the question of being. It is not evident how these analyses do so in *Being and Time*, but the rich analyses are certainly relevant to Kierkegaard's whole endeavor. As Kierkegaard himself says, there is the question of "repetition" for a religious individual; that is, "to what extent can an individuality, after having begun religious reflection, succeed in returning to himself again, whole in every respect?" (CA, 106) The authentic *Dasein* of *Being and Time* is not only authentic but also complete in its self-disclosure; it unifies its dealings with things and other people, its choice of historical engagement, and its understanding of being in general. Similarly, a religious man must be religious throughout his entire complex existence. One would thus expect Kierkegaard to say more than he does in a work such as *The Concept of Anxiety* about these multiple facets of being-in-the-world in terms of religious wholeness.

---

[24]*Being and Time*, H. 248.

This criticism may be directed more specifically at *The Concept of Anxiety*'s lack of discussion about mortality. Kierkegaard does not fail to mention it in the work; in one note, for example, he states that "the beast does not really die, but when the spirit is posited as spirit, death shows itself as the terrifying" (CA, 92). This is because death, like conception (orgasm) and birth, is an "anxious" moment for man because it is an extreme point of the synthesis at which spirit has nothing to do. In such a situation, the organic is primary, and spirit must simply let the organic run its course. His approach here is based, as one translator suggests, "on an ontological view of man, the fundamental presupposition of which is the transcendental reality of the individual, whose intuitively discernible character reveals the existence of an eternal component" (CA, xiv). Mortality, then, is not very important. However, it is unclear whether this assertion of man's eternality is, for Kierkegaard, phenomenological, merely speculative, or a matter of faith. Because of such uncertainty, Kierkegaard could have and should have given more serious consideration to mortality in his discussion of anxiety.

A similar criticism can be directed against the existential analytic of *Being and Time* when compared to the insights of *The Concept of Anxiety*. Repeatedly throughout the former work, Heidegger explicitly eschews any pretense of providing a complete existential analytic. He intends to analyze the being of *Dasein* only insofar as such analysis is necessary for clarifying and raising anew the question of being. One must assume, then, that what is put forth in *Being and Time* is all that is necessary for this endeavor, although there is no clue as to how Heidegger determines such necessity. If *Dasein* understands being in dealing with its own being and the being of other entities, it seems that the stages of psychophysical development, its sexuality, its intellectuality, as well as its "life of the spirit" may all have important bearing on its existence as the clearing of being. By ignoring such important aspects of being-in-the-world, *Being and Time* is guilty of important oversights in the analysis that it does provide.

For example, while Heidegger alludes to *Dasein* as a being that stretches out between birth and death, he does not acknowledge any qualitative differences in the phases of this process. The analysis thus gives the impression that a life at any stage between these termini either flees from its potential or appropriates itself authentically. One exists either as complete disclosure or as self-evasive partial concealment, and each of these existentiell modes presupposes that one has experienced anxiety as the uncanny disclosure of one's threatening freedom.

But even as disclosedness, man, as Kierkegaard points out, is a psychophysical entity undergoing development that conditions his capacity for disclosure in a variety of ways through the different phases of life. Hence, the anxiety of innocent ignorance, of childhood, is not that of the demonic individual who dreads freedom. It is milder, without guilt or suffering, and quite undetermined with respect to what one is able to do (CA, 42-46). Similarly, a distinction should be made between anxious innocence, anxious paganism, and the latent anxiety of spiritlessness. In all these cases, one could say that an individual is existing in some mode of self-"dis-integration," that he exists "inauthentically"; but all such activity cannot be accurately described as self-evasive. The latter occurs only under the conditions that enable what Kierkegaard calls a demonic life. Heidegger's analysis, however, does not acknowledge this qualification; on the contrary, if this essay's earlier comparison of fleeing everydayness to demonic inclosure is correct, then Heidegger recognizes only that anxiety Kierkegaard calls "anxiety about the good."

Because it glosses over important phenomenological distinctions in modes of anxiety, Heidegger's analysis distorts the existential phenomena of not-being-oneself. It may thereby also overlook questions pertinent to man's relationship to being. What, after all, is the significance of the individual's maturing process for his task of disclosing being? Is it merely extraneous to that task or has it some significance still to be explicated? That is, what does it mean that an individual must not only choose to realize himself, but must also exist for some years before he is even capable of realizing that a choice is to be made? Such questions are difficult at very best, but the richness of the phenomenon of human existence explored by Kierkegaard strongly urges their formulation.

To be sure, one must applaud the attempt of *Being and Time* to break through traditional notions of man and to think of him as disclosive, unified being-in-the-world; still, one cannot help but recall that man is still a psychophysical being-in-the-world, a disclosure or clearing of being that is essentially organic as well as spiritual (self-determining), an entity who, if he is a clearing, is not only a mortal one, but an embodied, sexual one as well. Might it not be crucial, in order to raise adequately the question of being again, to think about what such essential aspects of the clearing mean in relation to that for which it is the clearing?

Kierkegaard himself faces an analogous difficulty regarding the relation between the eternal aspect of oneself and sexuality. One may take issue with his intimation that a deepening love leaves sexual expression behind, but at least he attempts to come to terms with sexuality in his interpretation of existence. What does sexual embodiment contribute to the disclosure of being? Is it a mere reminder of a lower level of being? If an interpretation of disclosedness fails to consider this and other inescapable aspects of man's life, how seriously can one regard it? As much as *Being and Time* was able to appropriate and modify from *The Concept of Anxiety*, it seems that, with respect to the existential analytic, it should have learned more.

Tentative Conclusions and Larger Questions

Prior to the writing of *Being and Time*, Heidegger's thinking was influenced by his study of Aristotle, Augustine, Husserl, Dilthey, and Kierkegaard, among others. It is becoming clearer, however, that one of the most important influences on the existential analytic of *Being and Time* was Kierkegaard. It would even seem that from the preceding study of the aforementioned parallels and from Heidegger's own brief remarks, *The Concept of Anxiety* is the cornerstone of the relationship between the two thinkers. Furthermore, if one is interested either in Heidegger's quest for being or in an interpretation of human being, one could learn much from the corrective, complementary relationship that exists between the projects of these two men. But the task of thinking through the relationship between these endeavors goes far beyond what this essay attempts. It must deal, for example, with the later thought of

Heidegger as well as with Kierkegaard's other works. I will note only three major issues related to the above study upon which further efforts would have to focus.

First, this essay has only begun to explore the issue of anxiety. Heidegger carries his analysis much further, particularly in *What is Metaphysics*, where he all but identifies anxiety with what has often been described as "philosophic wonder." In this essay, he describes it as man's original encounter with being as such: "In the clear night of the nothing of anxiety the original openness of beings as such arises: that there are beings—and not nothing."[25] He describes it variously as a "peculiar calm," and a "bewildered calm" in which one experiences "a slipping away of beings as a whole." This, in turn, is related to "the anxiety of those who are daring," an anxiety that "stands . . . in secret alliance with the cheerfulness and gentleness of creative longing."[26] As Heidegger says in his postscript to this essay, "The clear courage for essential anxiety guarantees the mysterious possibility of the experience of being. Then close by essential anxiety as the terror of the abyss dwells awe. It clears and shelters that place of man's essence within which he remains at home in the enduring."[27]

One must ask how such description grows from and yet transforms the analysis found in *Being and Time*. One must then ask whether Kierkegaard's brief insights found in some of his notes about anxiety do not tend in the same direction. In a draft of *The Concept of Anxiety*, he notes that philosophy's beginning in wonder is a positive insight compared to the Hegelian notion of beginnings, but he does not connect this wonder with anxiety (CA, 170). Yet in an earlier note, he confides that "all existence makes me anxious, from the smallest fly to the mysteries of the Incarnation; the whole thing is inexplicable to me, I myself most of all" (CA, 170). This statement seems to be a presentiment of anxiety's alli-

---

[25]Martin Heidegger, "What is Metaphysics," in *Martin Heidegger: Basic Writings*, ed. David Krell (New York: Harper and Row, 1977) 105.

[26]"What is Metaphysics," 104-109.

[27]Martin Heidegger, "Postscript to 'What is Metaphysics,' " in *Existentialism From Dostoevsky to Sartre*, ed. Walter Kaufmann (New York: New American Library, 1975) 261.

ance with philosophic wonder, but Kierkegaard leaves it undeveloped. Does such anxiety disappear in faith or can one reconcile the latter with the later Heideggerian sense of anxiety? Is this later sense of anxiety phenomenologically verifiable or is it simply one possible interpretation of an experience open to several valid interpretations? These problems have yet to be worked out.

Second, how seriously must one take Heidegger's later assessment of Kierkegaard's work as entangled in metaphysics? In his letter on humanism, he asserts that "every determination of the essence of man that already presupposes an interpretation of being without asking about the truth of being, whether knowingly or not, is metaphysical."[28] As long as one sets man off "as one living creature among others in contrast to plants, beast, and God," one does not, according to Heidegger, think in the direction of man's essence. This statement would certainly apply to Kierkegaard's work, since he discusses man in relation to God without discussing the openness in which such an encounter can occur. He summarizes this thesis as follows: "the way that man in his proper essence becomes present to being is ecstatic inherence in the truth of being. Through this determination of the essence of man the humanistic interpretations of man as *animal rationale,* as 'person,' as spiritual-ensouled-bodily being, are not declared false and thrust aside. Rather, the sole implication is that the highest determinations of the essence of man in humanism still do not realize the proper dignity of man."[29] But, again, can one think and say the truth of being without coming to terms with man as "person" or as "spiritual-ensouled-bodily" being? Is it not perhaps the truth of metaphysics that is being appropriated when Heidegger, in various passages throughout his later work, speaks of man's "poetic" dwelling as the gathering of earth and sky, mortals and divinities, that is, as an existence grounded in the organic, intellectually reaching upward, self-conscious of its finitude, and sensible of the divine? And is it not precisely this truth that Kierkegaard addresses in his own

---

[28]Martin Heidegger, "Letter on Humanism," in Krell, ed., *Martin Heidegger,* 202.

[29]Ibid., 210.

way? Heidegger assures the reader that these interpretations are not to be thrust aside, but how they are to be incorporated still remains a mystery. The relation between the thinking of being and metaphysics, as well as between their respective approaches to existence, needs to be intensely explored in order to assess properly how the projects of the two thinkers in question ultimately stand in relation to one another.

Finally, and perhaps most importantly, one must explore the relationship between Heidegger and Kierkegaard in terms of faith, that is, in terms of the Judeo-Christian God and Christian salvation on the one hand, and of self-revealing and concealing being and its clearing on the other. For Kierkegaard, man achieves full self-integration through an act of faith in the God-man who delivers him from sin and who enables repentant, religious existence; for Heidegger, the homelessness of man as abandoned by being is overcome only by dwelling in the "homeland" of the "nearness of being." According to Heidegger, it is only "in such nearness, if at all, [that] a decision may be made as to whether and how God and the gods withhold their presence and the night remains, whether and how the day of the holy dawns, whether and how in the upsurgence of the holy an epiphany of God and the gods can begin anew." The holy as the essential sphere of divinity can radiate "only when being itself beforehand and after extensive preparation has been illuminated and is experienced in its truth."[30] According to Heidegger, one must think the truth of being to think the essence of the holy, and to think the latter in order to think the essence of divinity. Only then can one think or say "what the word 'God' is to signify."[31]

The issues here are perhaps the most complex of all and lead to the fundamental interpretive questions mentioned at the beginning of this essay. In one sense, one may interpret these different approaches to God as the difference that always exists between reason and faith, philosophy and theology. Yet Heidegger's thinking is not philosophical reasoning in any traditional sense, and

---

[30]Ibid., 218.

[31]Ibid., 230.

Kierkegaard's leap of faith, although it is a leap, is still allegedly supported by some intuitive sense of an eternal component in man. Is that which is signified by "God," at least in some sense, a mode of being's revelation or is "being" a detheologized version of the mystic's notion of God? How might one compare man's relationship to each? Can either of these interpretations encompass the other without remainder?

These are some of the central questions that must be explored if one cares to pursue a contemporary interpretation of human existence in light of these two thinkers. The task still lies before us.

Contributors

International Kierkegaard Commentary:
The Concept of Anxiety
Vincent A. McCarthy, Volume Consultant

LEE BARRETT is Assistant Professor of Theology at the Presbyterian School of Education

STEPHEN N. DUNNING is Associate Professor of Religious Studies at the University of Pennsylvania

LOUIS DUPRÉ is Professor of Religious Studies at Yale University

RONALD M. GREEN is the John Phillips Professor of Religion at Dartmouth College

RONALD L. HALL is Associate Professor of Philosophy and Religion at Francis Marion College

VINCENT A. McCARTHY is Associate Professor of Philosophy at Central Connecticut College

DAN MAGURSHAK is Associate Professor of Philosophy at Carthage College

ROBERT L. PERKINS is the Dean of the College of Arts and Sciences at Stetson University

ROBERT C. ROBERTS is Professor of Philosophy and Psychological Studies at Wheaton College

Advisory Board

Index